A Pitch for God

31 Baseball-Themed Devotions to Help You Live an Abundant Christian Life

by
Jim English

Table of Contents

Preface

This book is the culmination of many days and hours of contemplating the will of God in my life. After asking God what He wants from me, I concluded that God had called me to write this book for His honor and glory. It is my sincere hope that in some small way the words in this book will encourage and challenge you to consider the depth of God's abiding love for you.

I have chosen to explore spiritual truths through the lens of baseball for two reasons. First, like many fans of the game, I have a fondness for and pleasant childhood memories of playing baseball. Second, I believe spiritual truths are best understood when compared to common experiences or interests. This is essentially what Jesus did with the parables He used to teach about the kingdom of God. He used common occurrences in life to help people understand who God is, and how much He loved them by sending His Son to die for their sins. If baseball had been as popular then as it is today, I have no doubt that Jesus would have used baseball as a tool to foster faith in Him.

This book is not intended to be read in one sitting. On the contrary, it is my hope that each chapter will be read, discussed, and digested until you are ready to move on to the next chapter. I have concluded each chapter with the word "Selah" which I understand to mean "to pause and consider." Hopefully, that will serve as a reminder to pause and ask God what He is saying to you. The verses in each chapter are from the New International Version of the Bible.

Before you begin reading this book, ask God, by His Spirit, to reveal Himself to you like never before. I ask this because even though words are powerful, it is only when we have an encounter with God Himself that our lives will be forever changed.

Step into the batter's box. Here comes the first pitch.

The 1969 World Series Champions

There were 35 men who sought to do what no one else in their organization had ever done before. While all of them had the potential for greatness, there were only a few who were exceptional. On paper, their competition was better than they were, but paper is sometimes meaningless. Popular opinion expected the 35 to be defeated, but when the dust settled, victory became reality.

In 1969, the New York Mets won the World Series by defeating the heavily-favored Baltimore Orioles in five games.[1] The "Amazin' Mets,"a term given by their previous manager, Casey Stengel, did not allow their history to determine their future. What seemed impossible to others—namely, winning the World Series—became a reality on October 16, 1969.

The New York Mets became a National League franchise in 1962, and was part of a ten-team National League before they were placed in the National League East division.[2] From 1962 through 1968, the Mets had never finished higher than ninth in their division.[3] In 1969, the Mets won 100 games and lost 62.[4] They defeated the Atlanta Braves in 3 straight games before defeating the Orioles in five.[5]

The Baltimore Orioles packed a powerful punch in 1969. Led by manager Earl Weaver, the Orioles were 109-53, and

---

[1] retrosheet.org/boxesetc/1969/YPS_1969.htm
[2] en.wikipedia.org/wiki/1969_New_York_Mets_season
[3] Id.
[4] Id.
[5] Id.

finished first in the American League East division.[6] They had six all-stars, namely, Davey Johnson, Paul Blair, Dave McNally, Boog Powell, Brooks Robinson, and Frank Robinson. They also had three future Hall of Famers in Jim Palmer, Brooks Robinson, and Frank Robinson.

Some of the more notable Mets players included Tom Seaver, Nolan Ryan, Bud Harrelson, Tommie Agee, Ed Kranepool, Jerry Koosman and Donn Clendenon. Clendenon was named the most valuable player (MVP) of the World Series after batting .357 and hitting 3 home runs with 4 RBI.[7] Tom Seaver and Nolan Ryan would later be inducted into the baseball Hall of Fame.

****
Matthew 19:16-26

Many things in life seem impossible. What comes to mind when you consider the impossible? Is it peace in the world? Is it peace in your home? What about the mountain of debt that gets higher and higher? Jesus discussed impossibility with His disciples in Matthew 19:16-26:

> "Now a man came up to Jesus and asked, "Teacher, what good thing must I do to get eternal life?" "Why do you ask me about what is good?" Jesus replied. "There is only One who is good. If you want to enter life, obey the commandments." "Which ones?" the man inquired. Jesus replied, "'Do not murder, do not commit adultery, do not steal, do not give false testimony, honor your father and mother,' and 'love your neighbor as yourself.'" "All these I have kept," the young man said. "What do I still lack?" Jesus answered, "If you want to be perfect, go, sell your possessions and give to the

---

[6] retrosheet.org/boxesetc/1969/TBALO1969.htm
[7] en.wikipedia.org/wiki/1969_New_York_Mets_season

poor, and you will have treasure in heaven. Then come, follow me." When the young man heard this, he went away sad because he had great wealth. Then Jesus said to his disciples, "I tell you the truth; it is hard for a rich man to enter the kingdom of heaven. Again, I tell you, it is easier for a camel to go through the eye of a needle than for a rich man to enter the kingdom of God." When the disciples heard this, they were greatly astonished and asked, "Who then can be saved?" Jesus looked at them and said, "With man this is impossible, but with God all things are possible."

God made us in His image, and He has gifted men and women with the ability to do amazing things. From going to the moon to creating vaccines to inventing different communication devices, there seems to be no limit to what people can accomplish. But perhaps, we overuse the term "impossible" in our daily conversations. One example of that is how many people viewed the New York Mets in 1969. After winning the World Series, they were known as the "Miracle Mets."

A "miracle" is defined as "an event that appears inexplicable by the laws of nature and so is held to be supernatural in origin or an act of God."[8] Was the Mets victory over the Orioles inexplicable by the laws of nature? Of course not. The Mets played extremely well for four games with timely hitting and superb defensive plays to beat the heavily-favored Orioles, but it was hardly a miracle. Our words are prone to exaggeration when something unexpected happens. We tend to mischaracterize an extraordinary effort as a "miracle."

The disciples, along with others in their society at that time, considered the rich to be blessed and highly regarded by God. In the Old Testament (Deuteronomy 6:12-15), God had promised to prosper those who obeyed His law. The disciples

---

[8] thefreedictionary.com/miracle

probably thought that if anyone was going to heaven, it had to be the rich; otherwise, God would not bestow His blessings upon them.

With that thought in mind, it is no wonder the disciples were shocked and a bit dismayed when Jesus told them how hard it was for the rich to enter the kingdom of God. Essentially, Jesus told them that one of the reasons why this rich man would find it impossible to enter the kingdom of God was because he was trying to earn his way into heaven. Remember his question. "What good thing must I *do* to get eternal life?" Salvation and eternal life are gifts from God to those who have faith in Jesus. In the book of Ephesians, Paul tells us that salvation is not by works so no one can boast. (2:8-9).

In this world, nothing is free. All of us have to do something to get what we need to survive or enjoy the things we want. Because we live in a world where we have to work for what we have, we sometimes fall into the trap of believing we also have to work for our salvation. The truth is that no one can ever be good enough or do enough to deserve eternal life in heaven. It is a gift from God by His grace to those who believe in Jesus. If there ever was anything that was impossible for men or women to achieve, it is salvation. It required a perfect sacrifice to atone for our sins, and Jesus was and will be the only person that fits that description.

What are you working to gain from God? Are you laboring to persuade Him to love you? Do you work to be accepted by God or do you work because you have been accepted by God? The only work we must do to be accepted by God is to believe in His Son, Jesus Christ. (John 6:29). If we are doing good works to be accepted by God, we are destined for failure. We can never do enough to atone for our sins, and as we strive to earn our salvation, we will eventually burn out and give up.

Find rest and comfort in the fact that Jesus has done the work. Our job is simply to believe and obey. The 1969 Mets were amazing, but Jesus paid the price for our sins on the cross and won the victory for all of us by rising from the dead. Instead of remembering the "amazing Mets," maybe we should remember our "amazing Jesus."

Selah.

2

The Sacrifice Hit

In major league baseball, a sacrifice bunt is credited to a batter who successfully advances one or more runners by bunting the ball for an out.[9] A sacrifice fly is another type of sacrifice play which is now considered to be different from a sacrifice hit. Because the rules on exactly what constituted a sacrifice hit have varied over the years, the totals cannot be precisely compared.

Despite the differing definitions over the years, the clear leader for career sacrifice hits is Eddie Collins.[10] Collins played from 1906 to 1930 for the Philadelphia Athletics and Chicago White Sox.[11] Over his career, he amassed a total of 512 sacrifice hits.[12] His nearest competitor was Jake Daubert with 392.[13] Daubert played from 1910 to 1924.[14] In case these names are unfamiliar to you, let me compare Collins' numbers with a familiar name. Ty Cobb is twelfth on the sacrifice hits list with 295. The closest modern-day player is Tom Glavine who appears on the list as 69th with 216 sacrifice hits.[15]

You may wonder why all this fuss about sacrifice hits, in particular, sacrifice bunts. If you think about it, the sacrifice bunt is the most unselfish thing a baseball player can do. The player willingly forfeits his opportunity to hit so that another

---

[9] en.wikipedia.org/wiki/Sacrifice_bunt
[10] baseball-almanac.com/hitting/hisachit1.shtml
[11] baseball-almanac.com/players/player.php?p=collied01
[12] baseball-almanac.com/hitting/hisachit1.shtml
[13] Id.
[14] baseball-almanac.com/players/player.php?p=daubeja01
[15] Id.

player can advance to another base to put him in scoring position. In today's game, we rarely see players bunt sacrificially. This may be because the strategy of the game has changed, and because there seems to be a focus on hitting home runs. For the purist, it is a joy to see a player who can effectively bunt the ball for a hit or as a sacrifice to advance a teammate to another base.

****

Romans 12:1

The idea of sacrifice is an uncomfortable one when you consider how it is defined. One definition of "sacrifice" is "the act of giving up something highly valued for the sake of something else considered to have a greater value."[16] From this definition, it appears that when someone makes a sacrifice, there is a clear winner and a clear loser. The person who is giving something up appears to be the loser, and the person who is determined to be of greater value appears to be the winner.

A practical example would be helpful. Let's say your mother works two jobs so you can go to college. Your mother sacrifices time and money she could be spending on herself to help you pay your college tuition because she believes sending her child to college is of greater value than meeting her own needs.

Or, let's say a soldier falls on a grenade to save the lives of his fellow soldiers. This would be an extreme example of sacrifice in that it results in the loss of life. Why would a soldier make such a sacrifice? He believed the lives of his fellow soldiers were of greater value than his own.

---

[16] thefreedictionary.com/sacrifice

Some people might argue there seems to be a clear winner and loser in both examples. The ones who sacrificed something (the mother and the soldier who lost his life) are the losers, and the ones who gained something (the child and the other soldiers) are the winners. To those who believe this way, the attractiveness of sacrifice depends on whether they are the ones giving something up or the ones who are receiving a benefit because they were considered to be of greater value. Is there a clear winner and loser here?

From personal experience and from what we read in the Bible, we know there are no losers when someone sacrifices for another. Both are winners. Parents know this all too well. There is joy and contentment in knowing you have sacrificed your time or money to help your children have a better life. Parents do this because they love their children and see the lives of their children as more important than their own. Ask any responsible parent, and he or she will tell you they have no regrets for having sacrificed for their children.

The Bible has plenty to say about sacrifice. To avoid overwhelming you, I will only refer to a few verses that command us to put God and the needs of others before our own.

> "Be imitators of God, therefore, as dearly loved children and live a life of love, just as Christ loved us and gave himself up for us as a fragrant offering and sacrifice to God." —Ephesians 5:1-2

> "Your attitude should be the same as that of Christ Jesus: Who, being in very nature God, did not consider equality with God something to be grasped, but made himself nothing, taking the very nature (or form) of a servant, being made in human likeness. And being found in appearance as a man, he humbled himself and became obedient to death—even death on a cross!" — Philippians 2:5-8

"Then Jesus said to his disciples, "If anyone would come after me, he must deny himself and take up his cross and follow me. For whoever wants to save his life will lose it, but whoever loses his life for me will find it. What good will it be for a man if he gains the whole world, yet forfeits his soul? For the Son of Man is going to come in his Father's glory with his angels, and then he will reward each person according to what he has done." —Matthew 16:24-27

"Therefore, I urge you, brothers, in view of God's mercy, to offer your bodies as living sacrifices, holy and pleasing to God—this is your spiritual act of worship." —Romans 12:1

To be a Christian means to be Christ-like. The Bible uses Jesus Christ's sacrifice as the basis for reminding and commanding us to live a life characterized by sacrifice. When a person becomes a Christian by confessing his sins and putting his trust in Jesus as Savior and Lord of his life, the person is surrendering his will to the will of God. Some people want Jesus to save them from their sins so they can go to heaven someday, but to those who take this commitment seriously, there is much more. Jesus is not just Savior, He is also Lord of the universe and Lord of the individual.

Doesn't this mean that His plans and desires for my life take precedence over my plans and desires? The question is no longer "What do I want to achieve and do with my life?" Now, the questions are "What does the Bible say about how I should live, and what does God want me to do?" If we continue to hold onto our lives instead of surrendering them to God, we will live selfish, unsatisfying lives on earth, and eventually, we will be judged for rejecting God.

Jesus is our example of sacrifice. While we were still sinners, Christ died for us. (Romans 5:8). He gave up the peace and joy of heaven to come to a sin-filled earth to die for our sins so the believer could live eternally in heaven with Him. It seems to me that the very least we could do in return is to live our lives as He wants us to. This includes surrendering our will to His will and sacrificing for others. To put it in baseball terms, Jesus' sacrifice was a sacrifice home run for us, and our sacrifice for Him is merely a bunt that advances the runner.

Is sacrifice an attribute of my character? Is God asking me to put the needs of someone else before my own? How can I show the love of God to my family and others by serving them? Do I need to ask God to forgive me for being selfish? These are just a few questions we might consider as we remember Jesus' sacrifice for us.

Selah.

3

Is Anyone Keeping Score?

Everything on the baseball field is recorded. If a player wants to hide a bad performance, then he better not play baseball. A list of some of the activities recorded in baseball will be a helpful reminder:

- the teams who played
- the location of the game
- the result
- the players who participated in the game
- hits
- errors
- stolen bases
- the number and type of pitches thrown
- earned runs versus unearned runs
- when a batter reaches base on a fielder's choice, and
- whether a pitch was considered a wild pitch or a mistake by the catcher, referred to as a passed ball.

This data is used, in part, to calculate a team and pitcher's earned run average, a team's fielding percentage, a batter's batting average, his slugging percentage and his OPS (on base plus slugging percentage).

If this list does not convince you that everything is recorded, the list goes on. If you watch a television broadcast of a major league baseball (MLB) game, you will hear someone keeps statistics on a pitcher's record against a particular team, a particular batter, the percentage of times he throws his curveball and other pitches, the percentage of times his pitches result in a ground out or fly out, his record at home and on the road, his strikeout rate, etc. They keep similar statistics for batters that includes the batter's average against a particular pitcher, how often he has faced that pitcher and how many home runs he has hit against the pitcher. The list goes on and on.

You may wonder who it is that records all of this information. There is an interesting history behind who decides, for example, if a ball put in play is a hit, an error, or a fielder's choice. In the early years of baseball, the official scorer of this information was usually the sportswriter for the local newspaper.[17] It wasn't long, however, before there was criticism about scoring decisions that were widely believed to favor the home team. For example, some historians have questioned some of the local decisions made in New York giving Joe DiMaggio a hit that calls into question his 56 consecutive-game hitting streak.[18]

In 1953, Al Rosen narrowly missed being named a triple crown winner for his hitting when a questioned error caused him to finish one hit short of winning the American League batting title. Another controversy occurred in 1978 in the 8th inning in a game between the St. Louis Cardinals and the Philadelphia Phillies when Neal Russo, the official scorer for a local newspaper, determined a play to be an error rather than a hit. The St. Louis pitcher, Bob Forsch, went on to throw the first no-hitter of the 1978 season.[19]

In 1958, the Washington Post was the first newspaper to prohibit its sportswriters from being the official scorer in baseball games. After other newspapers followed suit, the MLB solved the problem by directly hiring official scorers for each stadium.[20]

---

[17] en.wikipedia.org/wiki/Official_scorer
[18] Id.
[19] Id.
[20] Id.

Have you ever thought about why baseball records all this data? What is the point? There are probably many reasons, but one reason that comes to mind is to determine which players should be rewarded and which should not. One such reward is determining who belongs in the Hall of Fame. Another more immediate reward is determining the salary that should be set for each player. It doesn't take much imagination to see how scorer decisions could affect how much money a player makes, and eventually, whether his statistics make him worthy of being inducted into the Hall of Fame.

****
Revelation 20:11-15; 22:12

Have you ever wondered if God is "keeping score?" Does God know everything we are going through and every good deed we are doing? Will He reward us for the good deeds we have done as long as they exceed the bad? I have heard of people who believe that as long as the number and weight of their good deeds exceed the bad, then they will enter heaven one day. To me, that sounds like a mathematical formula they have created, but is it God's formula?

We first have to begin with whether God knows all things. The word that is used to refer to this concept is "omniscience." The Bible has many verses that refer to God's omniscience, but I will only refer to two of them.

In Hebrews 4:13, the writer states,

> "Nothing in all creation is hidden from God's sight. Everything is uncovered and laid bare before the eyes of him to whom we must give account."

In Matthew 10:28-31, Jesus reminds us that God knows even the most insignificant details about us. Jesus states,

"Do not be afraid of those who kill the body but cannot kill the soul. Rather, be afraid of the One who can destroy both soul and body in hell. Are not two sparrows sold for a penny? Yet not one of them will fall to the ground apart from the will of your Father. And even the hairs of your head are all numbered. So don't be afraid; you are worth more than many sparrows."

While these verses in Hebrews and Matthew have a sobering aspect to them—namely, that we are accountable to God— they tell us that God knows all things and He is deeply concerned about each of us. Since we have established that God knows all things, the next question is whether He is recording this information like the official scorer in baseball and what He intends to do with the data.

Is God keeping a record of everything? If so, will He use this information to determine if a person enters heaven or hell or to determine what special rewards or punishment a person will receive?

Before we go any further, we need to clarify an important point. Whether we enter heaven or hell is not determined by deeds, but by what we believe. What I am referring to is what was discussed in Chapter One. The only people who will enter heaven are those who put their faith in Jesus Christ as cited in Ephesians 2:8-9. Salvation is a gift from God by His grace to those who believe.

God's Scorebook

There is a record mentioned in the Bible that is referred to as the Book of Life. In Revelation 20:11-15, the apostle John mentions the great white throne judgment where nonbelievers are judged for not having their names written in the Book of Life. The sentence for refusing to believe is to be cast into the lake of fire.

Moreover, God keeps a record of the good deeds performed by believers for the purpose of dispensing rewards in heaven. In Revelation 22:12, Jesus says,

> "Behold, I am coming soon! My reward is with me, and I will give to everyone according to what he has done."

This dispensation of rewards is consistent with God's fairness and goodness. Isn't it only right, for instance, that someone who has been active in sharing their faith, serving in the church and community, and helping others as they live out their faith should be rewarded more than someone else who has done much less? It is unwise to compare ourselves to others or judge their work for God, but it is safe to say we can trust God to fairly judge each person's work when deciding who should be rewarded for their service.

Judgment is serious business, and it has eternal consequences. But to put this in baseball terms, you and I don't have to worry about making it into God's Hall of Fame (heaven) as long as we have put our faith in Jesus Christ. It should be comforting for the believer to know that God knows all things because He, and only He, knows our hearts, and whether we truly believe and have put our faith in Him.

Conversely, it is important to remember that our works matter. They matter to those we help, and they will one day determine what "salary" (rewards) we will receive in heaven. While it is true that we are saved by grace alone, it is also true that we were created to do good works which God prepared in advance for us to do. (Ephesians 2:8-10).

Do you find comfort in knowing that God knows all things? The answer to that question may reveal the condition of your heart and whether you have put your faith in Jesus Christ as Lord and Savior. If you have, then ask yourself what good works God has called you to do.

If you have not put your faith in Jesus, then ask God to reveal Himself to you through the Bible, pray the prayer in Romans 10:9-10, and contact a local church to help you grow in your newfound faith. God yearns to save you and have a closer relationship with you. If you give God a chance, you will never regret it.

Selah.

4

27 Outs

In an average baseball game, there are 27 outs that must be collected before a game is completed. Three outs per inning for nine innings may not sound too difficult, but for those who have pitched a complete game, it can, at times, seem like an insurmountable task. It takes time, patience, and perseverance to get 27 outs to win a game. By the way, the all-time leader for pitching complete games is Cy Young at 749.

But this chapter is not about a pitcher at all. It is a story of an outfielder who persevered and never gave up on his dream to be a professional baseball player. His name is Daniel Nava.

In an article from History Locker, it was reported that when Daniel Nava entered high school as a freshman, he was 4'8" and weighed 70 pounds. When he graduated high school, he was 5'5" and weighed 150 pounds.[21] To say he wasn't the prototypical outfielder on his way to the major leagues would be an understatement.

When Daniel Nava was accepted at Santa Clara University, he was given the opportunity to walk on with the baseball team, but he failed to make the team. After deciding his prospects for a baseball career were dismal at best, he agreed to be the equipment manager for the team. Later, after being unable to pay his college tuition, he enrolled in a junior college and played for their baseball team. He played so well that Santa Clara came looking for him to offer him a full scholarship to

---

[21] historylocker.com/the-truly-inspiring-story-of-daniel-nava/

play baseball. Although he hit .395 in his only season with Santa Clara, he went undrafted in the major leagues. Refusing to give up on his dream, Nava played in the international league for the Outlaws of the Golden Baseball League. He performed so well that eventually his contract was bought by the Boston Red Sox. The purchase price for his contract was $1.[22] Apparently, the Red Sox did not have much faith in Nava, but it gave Nava the opening he needed to prove himself.

On June 12, 2010, at the age of 27, Daniel Nava made his first appearance in the major leagues as a member of the Boston Red Sox, and it was a memorable one to say the least. On the first pitch thrown to him, Nava hit a grand slam, making him only the second person in MLB history to hit a grand slam on the first pitch of his MLB debut.[23] In 2013, Nava had a .303 batting average, and he helped the Red Sox win the World Series that year.[24] Nava ended up playing approximately 7 years in the MLB before injuries shortened his career. Not bad for a one-time equipment manager.

****

Philippians 1:21
I Corinthians 9:24-25

For most of us, life is a long-distance run rather than a short sprint. To finish well in this life, we must have patience, perseverance, and the clearness of thought to never lose sight of our goals, like Daniel Nava. Can you imagine the disappointment he must have felt when he failed to make the Santa Clara baseball team? What was it like to become the team's equipment manager while still yearning to be on the field? Years went by before he had another opportunity at a junior college to prove himself. And as things were looking up

---

[22] Id.

[23] Id.

[24] baseball-almanac.com/players/player.php?p=navada01

for him after hitting .395 at Santa Clara, he again suffered disappointment by not being drafted.

A lesser person would have given up after failing to make the Santa Clara team the first time, but even after failing to be drafted, Nava continued his pursuit of being a professional baseball player. In the end, he was richly rewarded for his patience and perseverance. He played in 589 MLB games, had 452 hits, hit 29 home runs and earned himself a World Series ring in 2013.[25]

It is easy to be discouraged with life if we lose sight of why we are here and why we are doing what we are doing. For the Christian, our perspective should be like that of the apostle Paul who said in Philippians 1:21,

"For to me, to live is Christ and to die is gain."

This one sentence encapsulates our focus while on earth, and at the same time, directs our attention toward eternity. Everything we think, say, and do should reflect and revolve around our relationship with Jesus Christ. I have been guilty of compartmentalizing different aspects of my life. Maybe you have also. We tend to behave differently depending on what setting we are in. We talk and act one way at work, another way at the golf course, another way when our spouse is nearby and another way at church. Even Peter fell into this trap and had to be rebuked by Paul in Galatians 2. It seems to me that no matter where we are or who we are with, we should talk and act as people who love Jesus and want to serve Him and those around us.

You may be thinking that what I am suggesting is not attainable or sustainable for any length of time. That may be our past experience, but is that what God's Word says? Let's

---

[25] Id.

look at whether incorporating Jesus in every aspect of our lives is attainable.

In Philippians 4:13, Paul writes, "I can do all things through Christ who strengthens me." Does "all things" include living a life that honors God and allowing Jesus to live through us to touch the lives of those around us? The key to this verse is probably not "all things", but "through Christ." We know by personal experience and God's Word that, by ourselves, we can do nothing in our own strength. Jesus tells us in John 15:5 that apart from Him we can do nothing.

Paul tells us in 2 Corinthians 5:17 that "if anyone is in Christ, he is a new creation; the old has gone, the new has come." And again, in Romans 6: 6-7 he states, "For we know that our old self was crucified with him so that the body of sin might be done away with, that we should no longer be slaves to sin because anyone who has died has been freed from sin."

If we truly believe these verses, it seems that God is telling us that once we become believers in Christ, we are a new creation. Isn't a new creation one that did not exist before? Doesn't this mean that now that Jesus lives within us we have the power to not sin? Our former self, that body of sin, has been done away with, and we are free to live for God apart from the bondage of sin.

Is living a godly life sustainable over a lifetime? I think it is as long as we pray for God's help, daily surrender our will to His, and invite the Holy Spirit to empower us to do what we otherwise could not do. This process, which some refer to as sanctification, requires the same type of patience and perseverance exemplified by Daniel Nava on the baseball field.

Becoming what God wants us to be is a lifelong effort. God will do His part to help us be Christ-like, but we must do our part as well. It is a goal that is attainable with God's help and one that is well worth the effort.

Some people are always running away, but believers in Christ are called to run toward. Let me conclude this chapter with Paul's words in I Corinthians 9:24-25:

> "Do you not know that in a race all the runners run, but only one gets the prize? Run in such a way as to get the prize. Everyone who competes in the games goes into strict training. They do it to get a crown that will not last; but we do it to get a crown that will last forever."

Run for home where God can award to you the eternal prize He has prepared for you.

Selah.

5

Boston (617) Strong

On April 15, 2013, the Boston marathon was nearing an end when a bomb exploded near the finish line. The investigation showed that Tamerlan and Dzhokhar Tsarnaev were responsible for planting two pressure-cooker bombs near the finish line of the marathon. The blasts killed three people and injured approximately 280 others.[26]

On April 19, 2013, MIT police officer Sean Collier was killed trying to apprehend the Tsarnaev brothers who were in a stolen vehicle. Tamerlan was shot and killed as the brothers attempted to escape, and Dzhokhar was apprehended after being found hiding in a boat in Watertown, Massachusetts.[27]

On April 8, 2015, Dzhokhar was convicted in federal court on multiple charges and sentenced to death. As of this writing, his appeal remains pending.[28]

On April 16, 2013, the day after the deadly bombing, the Boston Red Sox played a game against the Cleveland Indians in Cleveland, Ohio. In the dugout before the game, the team displayed a jersey that read "Boston Strong 617." [29](The "617" represents the area code for Boston, Massachusetts.) A handwritten note by an unidentified Indians fan can be seen attached to a clipboard. The note read as follows:

---

[26] en.wikipedia.org/Boston_Marathon_bombing
[27] Id.
[28] Id.
[29] huffpost.com/entry/red-sox-617-jersey-note-indians-dugout_n_3100726

"From our city to your city: Our hearts and our prayers go out to you Boston. Love Cleveland."

Some days later, after the team returned to play at Fenway Park, David Ortiz walked to the middle of the field with a microphone in his hand and reminded those in attendance that no one was going to dictate the freedom of Bostonians. For a player who is likely to end up in the Hall of Fame, some believe this was Ortiz's greatest moment.

When the season was over, the Red Sox had won the American League pennant and defeated the St. Louis Cardinals in 6 games to win the World Series.[30] To this day, it is unclear whether the Red Sox players encouraged the Boston community to press on or whether the community, and in particular, the survivors, had inspired the players to win the title.

****

John 16:33
1 John 5:5
2 Corinthians 1:3-4

Tragedy and suffering oftentimes come without warning—a car accident, a diagnosis, a heart attack, a crime, the list goes on and on. Some tragedies affect a family while others affect a nation. The Boston bombings affected not only those who were injured and their families, but it affected our nation as well.

Other incidents of domestic terrorism have had a similar effect on our nation such as the April 19, 1995 bombing in Oklahoma City, and of course, 9/11. To say those events are in the past would be callous and insensitive. They still affect the nation as

_____

[30] retrosheet.org/boxesetc/2013/YPS_2013.htm

a whole today, especially the surviving victims and their family members.

Suffering takes many forms and has many causes, but one thing is certain. At some point in our lives, tragedy will strike. Jesus warned his disciples that there would be trouble in this world. In John 16:33, we read,

> "I have told you these things, so that in me you may have peace. In this world, you will have trouble. But take heart! I have overcome the world."

In John 14, Jesus, while talking to His disciples, talked more about peace. In John 14:27, Jesus stated, "Peace I leave with you; my peace I give you. I do not give to you as the world gives. Do not let your hearts be troubled and do not be afraid." The apostle John tells us who it is that overcomes the world. In 1 John 5:5, he writes,

> "Who is it that overcomes the world? Only he who believes that Jesus is the Son of God."

Where do we obtain peace? How can I overcome the loneliness and emptiness caused by the loss of a loved one? How do I deal with my fear of living in a dangerous and violent world? The answer to all of these questions is found only in Jesus.

It is only because of Jesus that mankind can now have a personal relationship with God. When Jesus died for our sins and rose from the dead, He reconciled to God those who choose to put their faith in Jesus as their Lord and Savior. Remember, Jesus told His disciples, and us, in John 16:33 that it is only in our relationship with Him that we can have peace.

We can seek peace in people, money, home-security devices, or weapons, but true peace can only be found when we are convinced where we will spend eternity. It is only the true believer in Jesus that can rightfully find rest and peace in this world. Once you know that heaven is your destination, the things of this life become less important.

You may be thinking that premise is fine when you experience anxiety over your personal safety, but the fact that you are going to heaven does not help you overcome the grief you feel over the loss of a loved one. I believe the answer is still found in Jesus. Let me explain.

In 2 Corinthians 1:3-4, Paul states,

> "Praise be to the God and Father of our Lord Jesus Christ, the Father of compassion and the God of all comfort, who comforts us in all our troubles, so that we can comfort those in any trouble with the comfort we ourselves have received from God."

If God is a God of compassion, and He is, what better time would there be for Him to show His compassion and comfort to us than when we are suffering? The scripture tells us that God comforts us in *all* our troubles. God is not too busy or so distracted that He fails to see what we are going through. We may convince ourselves that our problem is not big enough to deserve God's attention, but the size of the problem is immaterial. Whether it feels like it or not, God loves us and is concerned about every aspect of our lives. He wants to comfort us if we will only have faith to believe and ask for it.

There is another reason why God wants to comfort and help us. We see this in verse four. He wants us to take what He has given us and share that same comfort with others who are suffering or in trouble. We see this biblical truth come to life in the secular world.

How often do we read about someone who has endured a tragedy working as a volunteer to help others who are in a similar situation? Who is in a better position to help, for instance, a human trafficking victim than someone who was rescued from that life? In those cases, the person who has been rescued has far more credibility than someone who has not been a victim of that crime, and as a result, is more likely to gain the victim's trust. That is not to say that we have to go through the exact same thing others have gone through before we can help them, but when we have had a similar experience, it enhances our ability to help them through it.

Many times grief turns into anger, and that anger often is directed at God. We tend to question God's goodness by asking why a loving God would allow suffering and tragedy to flourish. No one knows why everything happens the way it does, but we know who we can trust to help us through it. His name is Jesus.

What trials and difficulties are you facing? What are you worried about that steals your peace? What are you doing to share with others the same comfort that God comforted you with? These are important questions to ask ourselves. It is easy to get so wrapped up in our own problems that we forget to go to the One who can help us. Whether your problems stem from a personal tragedy or from a national event like the Boston bombing, God is the help we need. All we have to do is ask Him and keep asking for His help and comfort. And after He has comforted you, follow the example of the Boston Red Sox—be a source of comfort to others who are suffering.

Selah.

6

The Black Sox Scandal

In 1919, the Chicago White Sox and the Cincinnati Reds met in a best of nine World Series. The White Sox were 88-52 that year while the Reds went 99-44. The owner of the Chicago White Sox was Charles Comiskey, and although the White Sox had the largest team payroll in 1919, it was rumored that the players disliked Comiskey because they believed he was underpaying them.[31]

At that time in the history of the sport, a player had to have a contract with a team to play professional baseball. Any player who refused to sign a contract was prohibited from playing professional baseball on any other team. Players could not change teams without permission from their current team, and without a player's union, the player had no bargaining position. The reserve clause in each player's contract stated that once his contract expired, the team retained their rights to the player. This meant that once a player signed a contract, the team, at its discretion, could reassign, trade, sell, or release the player.

Though bound by a contract that significantly favored the owner, some players found a way to make more money. Gamblers were known to pay off certain players to fix specific games, but what happened in 1919 was unique in that it was rumored that the entire World Series would be fixed in exchange for cash to be paid to specific players.

---

[31] en.wikipedia.org/wiki/Black_Sox_Scandal

It was believed that C. Arnold "Chick" Gandil, a first baseman with the White Sox, met with a gambler named James "Sport" Sullivan to work out the details.[32] Gandil allegedly enlisted the help of White Sox pitchers Eddie Cicotte and Claude "Lefty" Williams, shortstop Charles "Swede" Risberg and outfielder Oscar "Happy" Felsch. Third baseman Buck Weaver was reportedly in on the early stages of the plot, but he later declined to participate in the scheme. Utility infielder Fred McMullin was allowed to participate but only after he threatened to report the scheme after hearing about the conspiracy. "Shoeless" Joe Jackson was approached about the plot, but the extent of his involvement remains unclear.[33] His World Series batting average of .375 suggests he may not have been an active participant.

The purported arrangement was that after each loss the players would receive $20,000 in cash to be distributed among themselves. By October 6th, Cincinnati was winning the series 4 games to 1. Under the agreement, $80,000 should have been paid to the alleged conspirators, but it was rumored that the gamblers were behind on their payments. The players became angry, and allegedly decided to call off the scheme. The White Sox won the next two games, but the series went to the Reds when the White Sox lost game eight. The series ended with the Reds winning 5 games to 3.[34]

It wasn't until August 1920 that a grand jury convened to investigate a possible fix of another game that their attention turned to the 1919 World Series. Eddie Cicotte decided to testify before the grand jury, and he confessed to his participation in the scheme. Later, Shoeless Joe Jackson reportedly admitted to receiving $5,000 from his teammates, and Lefty Williams and Oscar Felsch confessed to their involvement. In October 1920, Gandil, Cicotte, Williams,

---

[32] history.com/news/the-black-sox-baseball-scandal-95-years-ago
[33] Id.
[34] Id.

Risberg, Felsch, Weaver, McMullin and Jackson were indicted on nine counts of conspiracy. The 8 members became known as the Black Sox. On August 2, 1921, the players were found not guilty, in large part, because all of the paper records relating to the grand jury confessions mysteriously disappeared.[35]

The story did not end there. Judge Kenesaw Mountain Landis, newly appointed as baseball's first commissioner, permanently banned the 8 Black Sox from professional baseball. The decree effectively destroyed their baseball careers.[36]

****

James 1:13-15
1 Timothy 6:6-10
1 Corinthians 10:13

Temptation is something everyone faces, and it is specific to each person. What is tempting to one may not be tempting to another, but the fact remains that everyone is tempted. Becoming a Christian will not exempt you from temptation. Even Jesus was tempted just like we are, but He never sinned by acting on that temptation. (Hebrews 4:15). Let's be clear. It is not a sin to be tempted. However, it becomes sin when we fail to resist the temptation, and we do what we are tempted to do.

James describes temptation and sin in these terms:

> "When tempted, no one should say, 'God is tempting me.' For God cannot be tempted by evil, nor does He tempt anyone; but each one is tempted when, by his own evil desire, he is dragged away and enticed. Then, after desire has conceived, it gives birth to sin; and sin,

---

[35] Id.
[36] Id.

when it is full-grown, gives birth to death." (James 1:13-15)

The motivation for the Black Sox to lose was to acquire money. Was the desire to obtain more money a sin? Probably not. Does the desire for more money become a sin when I act on that desire and do something to acquire it? That depends on what I do and how I go about obtaining more money. If I steal the money, then it is obviously a sin. What if my desire for money causes me to work 18 hours a day, and I am so obsessed with getting more money that I neglect my family and church? Have I now committed a sin?

We would all probably agree this example is not as clear-cut as the theft of money example, but some people would say this is also a sin. In the second example, it appears that money has now become an idol in my life. God expects us to put Him first on our list of priorities. We know this because Jesus taught that the first and greatest commandment is to love God with all of your heart, mind, soul, and strength (Mark 12:30).

Paul instructs Timothy on how we should regard money in 1 Timothy 6:6-10:

> "But godliness with contentment is great gain. For we brought nothing into the world, and we can take nothing out of it. But if we have food and clothing, we will be content with that. People who want to get rich fall into temptation and a trap and into many foolish and harmful desires that plunge men into ruin and destruction. For the love of money is a root of all kinds of evil. Some people, eager for money, have wandered from the faith and pierced themselves with many griefs."

Consider the 8 Black Sox players I referred to earlier. For those who accepted a bribe, they 'pierced themselves with many griefs' by being indicted, having their names and reputations tarnished, and being permanently banned from baseball. Even Buck Weaver, who may very well have been innocent of the charges, got caught up in the scandal by simply being associated with those who were guilty. The love of money can cause untold damage to the person involved and to those on the periphery such as family members, friends or church members.

I have only mentioned the love of money as a temptation that many people wrestle with, but there are a myriad of temptations in this world. We tend to think of the "evil" temptations such as jealousy, envy, theft, murder, fornication, pornography and the like. But there are many "innocent" temptations that are more subtle, such as the temptation to worry, fear, feel sorry for ourselves, or make excuses for our children to help them avoid being held accountable for their conduct.

What is a temptation for you? Take a moment to evaluate your life. Remember it is not a sin to be tempted. It is how we respond to that temptation that determines whether we sin.

It would be wise for all of us to be aware of our weaknesses so we can avoid temptation whenever possible. In those times where temptation is unavoidable, we can follow Jesus' example in Luke 4 when He was tempted in the desert. We can also hold fast to the promises in 1 Corinthians 10:13:

> "No temptation has seized you except what is common to man. And God is faithful; he will not let you be tempted beyond what you can bear. But when you are tempted, he will also provide a way out so that you can stand up under it."

God wants us to resist the temptation to sin, and He will help us in our weakness if we ask Him. In those times where we do sin, we should repent of our sins and trust in God to forgive us of our sins and cleanse us from all unrighteousness. (I John 1:9). Be encouraged in your fight against temptation. God is an ever-present help in our time of need (Psalm 46:1).

Selah.

7

Play by the Rules

A serious student of baseball will eventually consult the official rules of baseball. Prior to writing this book, I had never read the official rules, but when I did, the detail and specificity were quite overwhelming. In one chapter alone, the rules cover the layout of the field, the dimensions of home plate, the bases, the pitcher's mound, the catcher and batter's boxes, and the minimum distance the benches are to be placed from the baselines.[37]

Rule 2.01 states, in part, "The infield shall be a 90-foot square. The outfield shall be the area between two foul lines formed by extending two sides of the square... A distance of 320 feet or more along the foul lines and 400 feet or more to center field is preferable... The infield and outfield, including the boundary lines, are fair territory and all other area is foul territory." Rule 2.01 further states "The foul lines and all other playing lines indicated by solid black lines shall be marked with paint or other non-toxic and non-burning chalk or other white material."[38]

Of course, if you have rules, someone must enforce them. Major League Baseball has the general authority for enforcing compliance with the rules, but game decisions are left to the umpires. Rule 8.01(a) states "The umpires shall be responsible for the conduct of the game in accordance with these official

---

[37] content.mlb.com/documents/2/2/4/305750224/2019/Official_Baseball_Rules_FINAL_.pdf
[38] Id.

rules and for maintaining discipline and order on the playing field during the game."[39]

I came across a few interesting facts and a poem about umpires that I thought I would share with you. Only three umpires have umpired in more than 5,000 MLB games: Bill Klem, Bruce Froemming, and Joe West.[40] There have been 39 MLB players that went on to become an umpire, the last of which was Bill Kunkel.[41] Here is the poem I promised. It is entitled "The Umpire" by Milton Bracker.

"The umpire is a lonely man
Whose calls are known to every fan
Yet none will call him Dick or Dan
In all the season's games.

They'll never call him Al or Ed
Or Bill or Phil or Frank or Fred
Or Jim or Tim or Tom or Ted
They'll simply call him names."[42]

****

John 16:7-8,13
Psalm 19:12,14

No one likes to be held accountable. It hurts, or is, at least, uncomfortable to be confronted with something you have done wrong. When confronted, it is human nature to get defensive and, perhaps, argue with the person who is taking you to task for your error. Police officers encounter this on a daily basis. Baseball umpires do as well. We have seen numerous incidents where managers or players argue, scream, and curse umpires for what may or may not have been an incorrect call.

---

[39] Id.
[40] en.wikipedia.org/wiki/Umpire_(baseball)
[41] baseball-almanac.com/umpires/umpireswhowereplayers.shtml
[42] baseball-almanac.com/poetry/po_ump.shtml

But where would the game be without an umpire to make the decisions necessary to enforce the rules to ensure a fair outcome?

How does a police officer, judge, or an umpire know when a person has crossed the line? They have the rules memorized or they consult the rulebook. If I asked you 'For the Christian, where is the "rulebook"?', your answer would probably be the Bible. The Bible gives us several commands that guide and protect us while we are here on earth. It sets boundaries for us, much like the foul lines in baseball tell us what is fair and what is foul.

Despite the fact that there are over 1,000 commands in the New Testament, the Bible does not always clearly instruct us about what to do or not do. For example, the Bible does not tell you who to marry. It gives you general principles to follow, but it won't give you the name, address, and telephone number of your future spouse.

In those situations where we have to make a decision without clear guidance from the Bible, what do we do? What about those situations where we do something wrong but we don't realize it at the time? How do we become aware of incorrect thinking or wrong conduct? The Bible can help us with these questions. Let's look at a few verses.

The Holy Spirit is with us and in us to guide, teach, convict, and empower us to do the will of God. Shortly before Jesus' arrest, He had a long discourse with His disciples. In John 16:7-8,13, we read the following:

> "But I tell you the truth: It is for your good that I am going away. Unless I go away, the Counselor will not come to you; but if I go, I will send him to you. When he comes, he will expose the guilt of the world in regard to sin and righteousness and judgment; But when he,

the Spirit of truth comes, he will guide you into all truth. He will not speak on his own; he will speak only what he hears, and he will tell you what is yet to come."

The Holy Spirit provides us with the guidance we need when the Bible is silent on a certain issue. If we pray and believe He will guide us, the Holy Spirit will not let us down. The answer may not come immediately, but if we ask and continue to ask, we will find the answer we are looking for. He will also convict us when we sin so that once we are aware of it, we can repent and learn from our mistakes.

King David was concerned enough about committing unintentional sins that he prayed to God about it. In Psalm 19:12,14, David prayed,

"Who can discern his errors? Forgive my hidden faults... May the words of my mouth and the meditation of my heart be pleasing in your sight, O Lord, my Rock and my Redeemer."

Do you notice David's approach here? His prayer covers his thoughts, words, and actions, and he acknowledges he may go astray and not even realize it. This prayer tells God that David's utmost desire was to please Him, but he asks for forgiveness for those times when he unknowingly sins.

God wrote and preserved the Bible to help us know Him and to know right from wrong. He has also made the Holy Spirit available to correct and empower us to obey His will. Our culture today does not encourage people to obey what the Bible teaches. For example, does our society encourage submission to our rulers and those in authority? Does it look with favor on those who are humble and have a servant's heart? Does it reward those who are generous and unselfish? No, but God's Word does. Quite frankly, we have a choice to make. Will we follow society's rules, our own rules, or God's Word?

It takes time and effort on a daily basis to have a healthy relationship with someone. It is the same with God. We get to know God by communicating with Him and listening to what He has to say. We do this by spending time with God in prayer and reading the Bible.

If you have neglected God's word, then ask Him to forgive you. Let me encourage you to take at least 2 minutes a day to open your Bible and read what God has to say. If you do this faithfully, then 2 minutes will turn into 10 and 10 into 20. It will enrich and empower you to overcome the trials and tribulations of this world. It has for me.

Selah.

8

Play Between the Lines

In the previous chapter, I touched on the layout of the field as described in the official rules of baseball. In that chapter, I briefly described what is fair and foul territory. I found a website that graphically displayed in various diagrams the layout and dimensions of each MLB ballpark.[43]

As you can see from the diagrams, the distance from home plate to the left, center, and right field fences all vary as well as the height of the fences. For example, you will see that Fenway Park in Boston has the shortest distances to left, center, and right fields. The height of the right field fence at Fenway Park is the shortest in baseball, but the 37' fence in left field is the highest.

Despite these differences, you will notice from the diagrams that each park has designated foul line markers on the field and usually on the fence. One fact that varies in each ballpark is the amount of ground that a player can use to catch a foul ball. If you have seen a game in Oakland, California at what is now called Rickey Henderson Field, you will see a vast foul ball area versus a very limited foul ball area at Fenway Park.

As you already know, a foul ball has no value for the batter other than it forces the pitcher to throw another pitch and gives the batter one more opportunity to get a hit or a walk. I suspect foul balls have some value in the right situation, but in the big scheme of things, a foul ball is wasted effort.

43

reddit.com/r/baseball/comments/3kgrco/overlay_graphic_of_all_ml
b_field_dimensions

A player can hit a foul ball that, if fair, would have been a home run, but it is of no value. It only amounts to a loud strike. Or, a player could drop down a beautiful bunt where it would be impossible to throw out the batter, but if it rolls foul, it has no value. Baseball statistics cover everything imaginable, but have you ever seen statistics on how many times a player has hit a foul ball? There is a reason for that, and it is because foul balls, in large part, are meaningless.

In contrast, a hit has a plethora of benefits. It helps the batter get on base, it advances a runner, and it improves the batter's batting average. By the way, who is the all-time hits leader in baseball? If you answered "Pete Rose," you would be correct. He had 4,256. He is closely followed by Ty Cobb who had 4,189.

****
1Corinthians 13:1-7

While thinking about how meaningless a foul ball is, I began to wonder if there is something in life that is equally as meaningless. You are probably thinking that wondering what in life is as meaningless as a foul ball is pretty meaningless in and of itself, but please bear with me.

I began to turn my attention to 1 Corinthians 13. I will recite the correct version in a moment, but for now, I have adapted verses 1 through 3 to make a point and to make it more applicable to baseball.

> "If I can immediately distinguish between a changeup and fastball when the ball leaves the pitcher's hand, but all I can do is hit a foul ball, then my bat sounds like a resounding gong or a clanging cymbal. If I can predict what a pitcher will throw and even know what the pitch will be before the pitcher does, and if I have faith that I can hit a home run and win the game, but all I do is

39

hit a foul ball, then I have done nothing to help my team. If I use all my strength to get a hit or give up my right to hit by sacrificing a bunt, but all I do is hit a foul ball, then my batting average is not improved, and I gain nothing."

Now let's look at the text of 1 Corinthians 13:1-3:

"If I speak in the tongues of men and of angels, but have not love, I am only a resounding gong or a clanging cymbal. If I have the gift of prophecy and can fathom all mysteries and all knowledge, and if I have a faith that can move mountains, but have not love, I am nothing. If I give all I possess to the poor and surrender my body to the flames, but have not love, I gain nothing."

While wondering what activities are meaningless, I was reminded by Paul that our motives are the determining factor. King Solomon spent an entire book in the Bible considering the meaning of life, and he concluded that the whole duty of man is to fear God and keep His commandments. (Ecclesiastes).

But Paul's viewpoint in 1 Corinthians 13 may be preferable. He succinctly points to love as the defining difference between what is valued and accepted and what is not. Paul's words are almost poetic in how they bring to mind the most amazing, even miraculous, things a person could do and yet, how worthless they are unless they are motivated by love. I know if you are reading this, we all share a love for baseball. But even a baseball fanatic would have to agree that speaking the language of angels and moving mountains is a little more impressive than hitting a grand slam or throwing a no-hitter.

We know this truth from our own relationships, namely, that only those actions that are performed with love are acceptable. As an example, how would you feel if your spouse stayed married to you only because it was the right thing to do and not because he loved you? Or, what if your adult children came to visit you, not because they love you, but because they did not want to miss out on their inheritance? Neither situation would be acceptable and probably not tolerable for very long.

By the way, if you are wondering if by "love" I am referring to an emotional feeling or a commitment, then I will refer you to verses 4-7 in I Corinthians 13. The description of love in these verses is the kind of love we should demonstrate in all of our relationships, especially in our relationship with God. I wonder how many times we have gone to church, read our Bibles, or prayed out of a sense of duty rather than out of love.

If you are like me and you want to give your very best to God and others, then we should remember that love makes all the difference. It is probably healthy to ask ourselves from time to time what our motivation is for doing what we are doing. Is it to impress God? Is it to win the favor of others? Are we doing this to help someone or to make a good business contact? Am I doing this out of duty or out of love?

These are important questions to answer because the Bible tells us that even if we do great things, they may be of no value to us in the end if our motives are wrong. It may be of some value to others, but when God judges our work, it will be nothing more than another foul ball.

Selah.

9

Performance Enhancing Drugs (PEDs)

In February 2004, major league baseball announced a new drug policy that included random, off-season testing for players to determine if they were using performance-enhancing drugs. In November 2005, the players and owners agreed to stiffer penalties for violations of the drug policy, and those penalties were increased after the Mitchell Report was released on December 13, 2007.[44]

The Mitchell Report was written by former U.S. Senator George Mitchell who was commissioned by MLB commissioner Bud Selig on March 30, 2006 to investigate the extent of drug use in major league baseball. Selig became more concerned about the problem after reading a book entitled, "Game of Shadows" written by two reporters from the San Francisco Chronicle. The Mitchell Report covered the history of the use of illegal performance-enhancing drugs in baseball and the effectiveness of the MLB drug-testing program. The report listed 89 players who were alleged to have used steroids or PEDs.[45]

The current penalties, adopted in March 2014, include an 80-game suspension for a first offense, 162 games for a second offense, and a lifetime ban for the third offense.[46] My research showed that the only player who received a lifetime ban for using performance-enhancing drugs was Jenrry Mejia. He received an 80-game suspension for his first violation on April 11, 2015, a 162-game suspension for his second violation on

---

[44] baseball-almanac.com/legendary/Mitchell_Report.shtml
[45] Id.
[46] en.wikipedia.org/wiki/Doping in baseball

July 28, 2015, and a permanent ban for his third violation on February 12, 2016. The MLB drug policy allows players who have received a permanent ban to apply to the commissioner for reinstatement after one year. If the application is successful, the player may not be reinstated sooner than two years after the suspension began. Mejia applied for and was reinstated from his permanent suspension in 2018, and as of this writing, he was in the minor leagues after signing a contract with the Boston Red Sox.[47]

The extent of PED use makes you wonder why these amazing athletes would risk their health, a suspension, and loss of income to improve their performance on the field. I suspect the most common motives for using these drugs are money and the intense pressure the players feel to perform.

Baseball is performance-based, and part of the entertainment industry. If a player does not perform, he is benched, sent to the minors, traded, or released. All of these have financial consequences. The players know this better than anyone. Those who perform well are compensated well with long-term contracts while those who fail to perform are given shorter contracts if they are retained at all.

Players have a high-profile job that is examined and scrutinized not only by the fans and sports writers, but also by the front office of the team. Poor performance is not entertaining. If a team loses its entertainment value, then attendance drops and correspondingly, the team income drops. Once the team income begins to crumble, the roster gets adjusted, possibly leaving the non-performers out of a job.

There are many problems with the use of PEDs. First, it is cheating. Second, it tarnishes the integrity of the game. Third,

[47] en.wikipedia.org/wiki/Jenrry Mejia

it has health-related risks to the players that use them. Finally, it encourages the growth of an illicit industry that does more harm than good.

****
Ephesians 2:8-10

How important should performance be to the Christian? Do we have a duty to perform? Will a failure to perform jeopardize our Christianity and our relationship with God? Will God 'bench, send to the minors, trade, or release' those who fail to perform?

To begin with, we need to differentiate between salvation and the good works God has created us to do after we have become a Christian. We know that salvation is a gift of God's grace to those who believe. In Ephesians 2:8-9, we read,

> "For it is by grace you have been saved through faith— and this not by yourselves, it is the gift of God— not by works, so that no one can boast."

We cannot earn our way to heaven. It is a gracious gift from God to those who put their faith in Jesus Christ and the work He did by dying on the cross for our sins. God has done the work. Our job is simply to believe.

If we continue reading in Ephesians 2, we see that good works are part of God's plan for our lives. Verse 10 states,

> "For we are God's workmanship, created in Christ Jesus to do good works, which God prepared in advance for us to do."

God created us to have a relationship with Him, but this verse reminds us that God also created us to complete the good works He prepared for us to do. Once we become believers, God expects us to perform good works to help people and to show God's love to them. Therefore, it appears that we do have a duty to perform.

Will God 'bench, send to the minors, trade, or release' the Christian who fails to do the works God has prepared for him to do? In John 14-16, Jesus had a great deal to say about being fruitful and obeying His commands. In John 15, He described Himself as the vine, and believers as the branches of the vine. He used this illustration to show us that just as a branch is dependent upon the trunk for sustenance, we also can do nothing apart from Jesus. But if we love Him and strive to obey His commands, He will enable us to bear much fruit so that we can bring glory to God.

In John 15:2, Jesus tells us that God will cut off those that bear no fruit, but immediately after saying this, He states that He will help those who bear some fruit to be more fruitful. There is an important differentiation here between those who bear no fruit and those who are not as fruitful as they could be.

Most of us probably fail to see the good we are doing for the kingdom of God. If you are in that group and are feeling a bit nervous about being cut off by God, then consider this. If you did not care about your relationship with God and how you can help advance the kingdom of God, would you be reading a book like this? No. God loves us and wants us to fulfill our calling to do the good works He wants us to do. If this is true, then where do we get the strength and wisdom we need to do what God wants us to do? From the Holy Spirit.

The Bible has a great deal to say about the Holy Spirit and how He teaches, guides, helps, and comforts a believer. Here is a list of some of the verses that remind us how essential the Holy Spirit is in the life of a believer: Acts 2:38-39; Romans 8:14-16; Romans 8:26-27; John 16:7-13; and 1Corinthians 12:7-11.

Although these verses are powerful and true, there is possibly no better illustration of the power and benefit of the Holy Spirit than the life of Peter. Prior to receiving the indwelling presence of the Holy Spirit, Peter was, at times, impetuous, impertinent, and overconfident. On one occasion, he tried to tell Jesus what to do, and when he did so, he was firmly rebuked. (Matthew 16:21-23). He professed to be loyal to Jesus even unto death, but later, denied Him three times. (John 13:36-38; 18:15-27). When Jesus was being arrested, he drew his sword and cut off the right ear of Malchus, the servant of the high priest. (John 18:7-10). Yet again, Jesus had to curb Peter's zeal.

But we see a different Peter after his upper room experience in Acts 2. We now see a disciple who is courageous, faithful, powerful, and wise. There can be no other explanation for this transformation in Peter than the Holy Spirit. Not even the resurrection, by itself, can explain this transformation.

Prior to Acts 2, Peter was convinced that Jesus had risen from the dead, but it wasn't until the Holy Spirit came upon him that we read of the courageous preaching and astounding miracles that God performed through him. If we need an example of doing good works, Peter would be a good role model. He preached one sermon where approximately 3,000 people were saved (Acts 2: 40-41). His shadow was all the sick needed to fall on them to be healed (Acts 5:15). God used him to heal a man who was crippled from birth. (Acts 3: 2-8). He shared a brief message with Cornelius and his household, and the Holy Spirit filled all those in attendance. (Acts 10).

Thank God that, unlike baseball, our salvation is not performance-based. It is a gift of God's grace to those who believe. But it is also our privilege to do the work God has called us to do. God could supernaturally save the lost souls in this world, meet a financial need, or heal someone's body without our help. He has done and will continue to do those miracles in the future. But God predominantly uses people to help other people.

Why He would leave this important work to the frailties of mankind is debatable, but possibly, it is for our joy and His glory that He has assigned this task to us. Maybe, when others see us unselfishly helping them, they see the love and power of God at work in a tangible way. Moreover, there is no greater joy than helping someone who cannot return the favor. Is it possible that God knows what He is doing by preparing in advance good works for us to do?

How are we doing when it comes to doing the good works God has called us to do? How can I know what God wants me to do? If we ask God each day what He wants us to do for Him and for someone else, He will show us. As we take that step of obedience, we will see that that type of unselfish life is one that will be greatly rewarded in this life and in the life to come. And don't worry about having the wisdom and strength to do the work God has called you to do. We don't need PEDs to serve God. We have His Spirit abiding within us.

Selah.

10

The Art of Pitching

Deception and temptation are the bedrock of good pitching. Some might say that a 95+ mph fastball should be included on that list. A good fastball surely helps, but if you think about it, professional baseball players have proved themselves over and over again to be more than capable of hitting a fastball. It is only when they are deceived by a pitch or get caught looking for a breaking ball, that the fastball proves most effective.

In basic terms, a pitcher's goal is to get the batter to make an out in as few pitches as possible. He has to throw a five-ounce baseball that is 9-9.5 inches in circumference in such a way as to cause the batter to miss the ball or cause him to hit it to one of the pitcher's teammates. How does he do that? By deception and temptation.

Consider the different types of pitches that are thrown such as the curveball, slider, change-up, fastball, and knuckleball. There are also variations of some of these pitches. For example, some curveballs break in a 12 to 6 direction (using the face of a clock) while others break more from 2 to 8. Fastballs can be thrown in a manner where they either tail off to the right or to the left. The speed, spin rate on the ball, or absence of spin all affect where the ball will go and at what velocity. Since good pitchers throw each pitch from the same arm slot, it makes it very difficult for a batter to determine what pitch is being thrown. And when you factor in that a batter has about a quarter of a second to identify the pitch, decide to swing, and initiate the swing to hit a 90- mph fastball, pitchers can make life incredibly difficult for a batter.

That is probably why the old adage that 'good pitching beats good hitting' is generally true.

If you have ever heard a pitcher being interviewed on television, you have probably heard him say how important it is for him to avoid throwing the ball over the middle of the plate. This is because those pitches are the easiest to hit. Instead, pitchers strive to throw strikes over the edges of the plate, and they raise or lower the height of their pitches to force the batter to change his eye level. To be effective, they have to throw different pitches over different areas of the plate so the batter cannot predict what and where the pitch will be thrown. For example, if a pitcher throws 85% curveballs that routinely break over the outside corner, a batter will simply wait for that pitch and hit it. On the other hand, if a pitcher has 3 or 4 different pitches and mixes up the location, then the batter will have a more difficult time predicting what will be thrown and make the necessary adjustments to hit the ball.

Quite often, the pitch that seems to fool batters the most is the change-up. A batter may get accustomed to seeing a 90 mph fastball so when a pitch is thrown that does not have the spin, for instance, of a curveball, they assume this is another fastball that is coming at 90 mph. When, instead, it turns out to be an 82 mph change-up, the batter swings before the ball reaches the plate and misses the ball. To the fan, it looks like a slower and easier pitch to hit, but the batter is deceived by the speed of the pitch and misses it entirely. In this scenario, the batter sees a pitch that is tempting to hit, but he misses it because the pitcher has deceived him into thinking the ball is approaching the plate at a faster speed.

While curveballs, sliders, and fastballs follow a certain trajectory due to the spin on the ball, the knuckleball does not. One reason is because the knuckleball is thrown with no spin. With an absence of spin on the ball, it is largely affected by its velocity and the atmospheric conditions present in the ballpark. Batters, catchers, and pitchers often have no idea where the pitch will end up. Bob Uecker, a catcher in the MLB for six years, is quoted as saying that "the best way to catch a knuckleball was to wait until it stopped rolling and pick it up."

The inability to predict where this pitch will go makes it harder for the batter to decide whether to swing. The pitch may be out of the strike zone when it leaves the pitcher's hand, but by the time it crosses the plate, it is a strike. The speed of this pitch is not a problem for the batter. It is the unpredictable movement of the pitch that deceives him.

****

Matthew 4:1-11
Colossians 3:1-3

If deception and temptation were confined to the baseball field, we would live in a more pleasant world. Even people who know very little about the Bible know that deception and temptation were present in the Garden of Eden. Why God would allow Satan to enter the Garden to deceive and tempt Adam and Eve is an interesting question, but an inquiry that goes beyond what this chapter is about. The fact remains that deception and temptation are not something new that entered the world when the iPhone was invented. They have always been with us and will continue to be until we breathe our last breath or Jesus returns, whichever occurs first. Before we consider how to deal with the 'twin brothers of evil '(deception and temptation), let's consider how prevalent they are, what form they present themselves in our world, and how severe the consequences are when we are deceived and succumb to temptation.

The dictionary defines deception as "the act of causing someone to accept as true or valid what is false or invalid." The word is also defined as "the fact or condition of being deceived."[48] In other words, we can be on the giving or receiving side of deception. We can deceive others or we can be deceived by others.

Temptation is defined as "the act of enticing someone to do evil or the state of being enticed."[49] Again, we can tempt someone to do something wrong, or we ourselves can be enticed to do wrong. What is tempting to you may not be tempting to me. The Bible tells us that each person is tempted by his own evil desire. (James 1:14). Temptation, by itself, is not a sin, but when we act on that temptation, we sin. Jesus was tempted in every way we are, but He did not sin because He never yielded to the temptation. (Hebrews 4:15).

What are people tempted to do that is wrong or evil? The list is long and covers all the evil in the world, but let's make a brief list. How about hate, murder, theft, revenge, adultery, pornography, abducting children, assault of a spouse, and selling illegal drugs to high school students? We know these are tempting for certain people because we read stories about them on the internet or hear about them on a news broadcast.

But what about the 'white collar' temptations that are almost as evil and can hurt others? What about the temptation to curse someone out on Facebook or during a road rage incident; to not report a crime because we don't want to get involved; to criticize or gossip about someone we dislike; to be selfish and unfriendly to others because we are in a bad mood; to envy the wealth and possessions of others; and to ignore the poor and needy because they are too burdensome to deal with? The list of 'white collar' temptations may be more lengthy than the temptations we immediately think of as evil.

---

[48] merriam-webster.com/dictionary/deception
[49] dictionary.com/browse/temptation?s=t

What about deception? How prevalent is it in society? It is everywhere, even in our own hearts. In Jeremiah 17:9, the prophet stated, "The heart is deceitful above all things and beyond cure. Who can understand it?" I will mention places in society where we find deception, but we need to remember that we often deceive ourselves. For example, a husband may think his relationship with his wife is in good shape because that is what he wants to believe when, in fact, his marriage is in serious trouble.

Many crimes are crimes of deception. A dishonest bookkeeper can make it appear that the company's finances are in order, but the truth is the bookkeeper has been embezzling money for years. A person can present a counterfeit $20 bill to a cashier and purchase merchandise with worthless money. An elderly person can wire money to an unknown person he talked to on the phone only to discover he has been scammed into giving away his social security check.

Businesses, governments, nonprofits, and some religious organizations have been guilty of deceiving those they serve or who make financial donations. It is the same for plumbers, lawyers, doctors, financial consultants, teachers, you name it.

What damage is caused when someone is deceived or surrenders to temptation? Financial ruin, divorce, prison, public humiliation, suicide, disbarment, depression, addiction, and health problems to name a few. More often than not, it is not only the person who succumbs to temptation that suffers but his family and friends as well. The heartache and suffering associated with giving in to temptation probably are not fully considered when the tempting situation presents itself. It is not until it is too late that the person fully realizes the consequences of his or her misconduct. If we could see the end result from the beginning, then whatever is tempting us wouldn't be so tempting.

How then do we avoid being deceived and surrendering to temptation? We look to Jesus as our example. Jesus was tempted just like we are, but He never sinned. The form that temptation took may have been different 2,000 years ago, but He was tempted with the same issues of the heart that we are today. How did Jesus deal with temptation? By knowing and applying the scriptures, by knowing who He was, and by focusing on what God had called Him to do.

In Matthew 4 and Luke 4, we read about Jesus being tempted by the devil in the desert. He was tempted to meet his physical needs, to possess all this world has to offer, and to prove His identity as the Son of God. Some relate these temptations to what John referred to as the lust of the flesh, the lust of the eyes, and the pride of life (1 John 2:16).

Jesus resisted the devil and these temptations by reciting the Old Testament scriptures that related to each temptation. We tend to forget that the Word of God is a serious weapon. Hebrews 4:12 tells us, "For the word of God is living and active. Sharper than any double-edged sword, it penetrates even to dividing soul and spirit, joints and marrow; it judges the thoughts and attitudes of the heart." We may think of modern-day weapons, such as a gun, as being able to harm the body. Here we see the Word of God penetrates the body, soul, spirit, thoughts, and attitudes of the heart.

Moreover, there are several examples in the Bible that show us that Jesus refused to be distracted by anything that might deter Him from His mission to spread the gospel and to die for the sins of the world. Let me direct you to two examples.

In Mark 1:21-39, we read about Jesus performing several miracles that made Him more and more popular. When He was urged to stay where He was because of His increased popularity, He told His disciples He had to go to other villages to spread the gospel because that was what He was called to do.

In Matthew 16:21-23, after Jesus again predicted His death, Peter rebuked Jesus and told Him that would never happen. Undeterred from His calling to die for our sins, Jesus looked at Peter and told Satan to get behind him and to not interfere with God's plan for His life. Even one of His closest disciples could not prevent Jesus from doing God's will.

Finally, in John 13, we see that Jesus knew full well who He was, what His death would include, and where He was going before He washed the feet of His disciples. In verse 1, we read,

> "It was just before the Passover Feast. Jesus knew that the time had come for him to leave this world and go to the Father. Having loved his own who were in the world, he now showed them the full extent of his love."

If you think about it, knowing who we are (our identity) is crucial to avoiding deception and resisting temptation. This raises an important question. From where or whom do we get our sense of identity? Is it from our work, feedback from others on social media, our family and friends, Hollywood, or how we feel about ourselves? As I make this list, it seems those sources are dubious at best.

Instead of finding our identity from sources that may prove to be unreliable, shouldn't we instead look to the Bible to discover what God says He created us to do and be? If God tells me He loves me and I am his son, shouldn't I believe that over what others say about me? If God says I am forgiven, then maybe I should believe that and forgive myself as well. If God says I am holy, then shouldn't I believe that even though I don't feel holy? What do you think?

Before we leave this subject, let's look at other scriptures that can help us avoid giving into temptation. In Colossians 3:1-3, Paul states,

> "Since, then, you have been raised with Christ, set your hearts on things above, where Christ is seated at the right hand of God. Set your minds on things above, not on earthly things. For you died, and your life is now hidden with Christ in God."

Desiring and thinking about spiritual things over the things of this world will go a long way in helping us avoid being deceived and committing sin by giving in to temptation. Deception and temptation first pass through our minds, then into our hearts, and finally, by our actions. If we can protect our minds and hearts by focusing on God and what He has called us to do, then we will avoid the sinful actions that hurt God, others, and ourselves.

Verse 3 was always perplexing to me when I read "your life is now hidden with Christ in God" until a pastor explained it this way. He put a dollar bill in his Bible and closed the Bible so that all we could see was his Bible. He then said we are like the dollar bill. When God looks at us, He sees only Jesus and His righteousness. Because of the work Jesus has done, we are now in a position to set our minds and hearts on God and not on the things of this world.

Good pitching is based on deception and tempting the batter to swing at an unhittable pitch. No batter enters the batter's box without experiencing deception and temptation. The world is our batter's box, and we too, without fail, will encounter deception and temptation. If we think we are above being deceived, we have already been deceived.

But we are not without help. The Holy Spirit will guide, teach, and help us avoid the perils associated with temptation and deception. We can rely on the promises in the Bible to help us, and we should look to Jesus as our example for how to defeat sin. Ask God each day to give you a discerning spirit to help you see right from wrong and to keep you on the right path. That is a prayer God wants us to pray and one He wants to answer.

Selah.

11

The Hall of Fame

The National Baseball Hall of Fame and Museum is located in Cooperstown, New York. The first class of Hall of Famers was elected in 1936, and the inaugural ceremony was held on June 12, 1939. The first class consisted of Ty Cobb, Walter Johnson, Christy Mathewson, Babe Ruth, and Honus Wagner.[50] Through 2018, there have been 329 people elected into the Hall of Fame: 261 players, 23 managers, 10 umpires and 35 pioneers and executives.[51]

How does a person get selected to be a member of the Hall of Fame? Generally, it is the active and honorary members of the Baseball Writers' Association of America who elect candidates into the Hall of Fame. A player must have played at least 10 years in the major leagues, and he must have retired from baseball for 5 years to be eligible to be on the ballot. Any candidate receiving votes on at least 75% of the ballots cast is elected into the Hall of Fame.

The top five voting percentage recipients as of early 2019 were Mariano Rivera, Ken Griffey, Jr., Tom Seaver, Nolan Ryan, and Cal Ripken, Jr. Mariano Rivera is the only person in major league baseball history to receive 100% of the votes on the ballots cast. By the way, Babe Ruth is 16th on that list.[52]

The Hall of Fame is reserved for the best of the best in baseball, but performance on the field is apparently not the

---

[50] en.wikipedia.org/wiki/National_Baseball_Hall_of_Fame_and_Museum
[51] baseball-almanac.com/hof/hofstat.shtml
[52] baseball-almanac.com/hof/hofmem4.shtml

only consideration. The introduction of alleged steroid use, and in one case, gambling on the outcome of a game, have kept certain players from getting the votes they need to enter the Hall of Fame. The failure of these players to be inducted causes fans to theorize that more than statistics are required before a player receives this honor. Possibly, character and how a player played the game are prerequisites to enter the Hall of Fame, and rightfully so.

Consider for a moment how long and difficult it must be to enter the Hall of Fame. A player begins playing baseball at 6 or 7 years of age, and if his health holds up, he plays until he is 35 or so. Once he makes it to the major leagues, he plays 162 games per year. He is not only constantly working on his swing and taking fielding practice, but he has to travel extensively and spend substantial periods of time away from his family. In fact, teams travel so frequently that some players look forward to retirement so they can finally spend time with their children. Don't get me wrong. That is a good reason to retire. But the feeling of absence from family only serves to accentuate the fact that players spend a great deal of time on the road.

On one hand, it is hard to feel sorry for players when you consider how much money they make and how famous they are, but there is a price they pay for playing baseball. Even though they spend all this time and effort on a baseball career, there is no guarantee the Hall of Fame will be their destiny. All this sounds pretty tiring so why do they do it? Why play professionally for, at the most, 20 years and then have to find a second career? They love the game, and they love to compete.

If you were a professional baseball player, what would you want your legacy to be? Would it solely be to make a ton of money? Or, would it be to be recognized as a player who did his best on every play in every game over your entire career?

Or, would you want to be seen by the fans and your peers as a winner and the type of player that made his teammates better as well? How about someone who is remembered as a good teammate who helped the less fortunate in the city where he played?

Although all of these are worthy goals, there are likely two baseball-oriented goals pursued by every major league player. First, to win a World Series. Second, to be inducted into the Hall of Fame. Some players reach one goal but not the other. Most never reach either. A few have reached both.

There have only been 143 players who won a World Series and later were inducted into the Hall of Fame.[53] That may sound like a high number to you, but when you consider that since 1871 there have been approximately 20,000 players in major league baseball, 143 represents only .715% of everyone who has ever played.[54] This means that less than 1% of all players have reached the elite status of having won a World Series and been inducted into the Hall of Fame.

****
Matthew 20:20-23
Mark 10:35-40

Have you ever wondered if there is an eternal 'Hall of Fame' for the Christian who performs at a high level akin to the one for baseball players in Cooperstown? Most of us would agree there is a heaven, but how believers will be recognized for their outstanding service and whether they will have a special place of honor are a bit more uncertain. However, there is scripture that supports the belief that there will be special places of honor for certain people.

---

[53] baseballhall.org/discover-more/stories/hall-of-famer-facts/hof-players-who-won-world-series
[54] baseball-reference.com/leagues/index.shtml

Do you remember the request made by the mother of James and John in Matthew 20:20-23? She knelt before Jesus and asked Him to place her two sons next to Jesus when He ruled in His coming kingdom. Looking back on this, two things come to mind. First, she may not have been specifically referring to heaven because it is widely believed that many of Jesus' followers believed Jesus would defeat the Romans much like a military conqueror would, and then He would establish His rule on earth.

Second, this should have been extremely embarrassing for James and John. Picture this. Your mom comes to your job and asks the president of the company to make you vice president. How could you ever face your boss or even your co-workers after that? They would probably be wondering if you put your mom up to that or even worse, that you were seeking a promotion based upon something other than merit.

My suspicion that this would be highly embarrassing for James and John would be correct if it were not for Mark 10:35-40 where we read about James and John personally making this same request. Reading these passages together leads us to only one conclusion. This must have been a family decision to petition Jesus to elevate James and John not only over the other disciples, but over every future believer in Jesus. Even if we give them the benefit of the doubt and assume this was simply poor judgment on their part, it is still a bit shocking.

What was Jesus' response to their request? He asked one question, and then He made a couple of statements. First, He asked if James and John could drink the same cup of suffering that Jesus knew He was about to experience by being crucified for a crime He did not commit. Second, He told them that they did not understand the magnitude of what they were asking. He told them (and us) that whoever sits on His right and His left in heaven is a decision to be made by God the Father. Imagine, not even the perfect Son of God makes that decision.

We do not know what criteria must be met to be given this place of honor, but we now know that there will be such a place. As special as it may seem to be inducted into the baseball Hall of Fame, it will be nothing compared to having the seat next to Jesus.

Before we conclude this chapter, I want to refer you back to some of my previous questions regarding what type of legacy you would like to leave if you were a baseball player. Instead of baseball, how about we rephrase those questions and have them relate to our life on earth. In other words, when you die, what do you want your legacy to be to those you leave behind? More importantly, how do you want God to see your legacy? What is the gift you want to leave your family and friends? What gift do you want to give to God?

Is it tremendous wealth? Is it the memory that you did the best you could as a parent, friend, citizen, and church member over the length of your life? Is it to be remembered as someone who made those around you better than they would have been if they had never met you? Or, is it to be remembered as someone who "played the game" right by living a life of integrity, compassion, and self-sacrifice to make the world a better place to live?

What gift can you leave God? What can you give God who has and owns everything? Perhaps, the only gift we can give God is a life that is devoted and committed to serving, worshipping, and honoring Him until we breathe our last breath. If you can honestly say you have lived a life devoted to God from your childhood, then thank God that He has blessed and helped you avoid a lot of pain and suffering. If you are not in that group, then there is still good news. To use a baseball metaphor, it is not where you are in the standings at the all-star break that counts, but where you stand when the season has ended. In other words, it is not how we begin life that is important, but how we finish.

Unfortunately, only some will surrender their lives to God. In His sermon on the mount, Jesus spoke of the wide and narrow gates in Matthew 7:13-14. He clearly tells us that most people will take the path that leads to destruction, but only a few will take the road that leads to life. If you are like me and you have had regrets about your past behavior, then there is still hope. To those in need of salvation, God has an open invitation for us to become children of God. Romans 10:9-10 tells us that if we confess with our mouths that Jesus is Lord and believe in our hearts that God raised Jesus from the dead, then we will be saved.

To those of us who have experienced salvation but have become complacent and fallen into bad habits, there is hope. God promises to restore those who confess and repent of their sins and to cleanse us from all unrighteousness. (1 John 1:9). Whether it feels like it or not, God loves us. He wants us to present Him with a life that is well-lived and one that brings honor and glory to Him.

No matter what your relationship with God is at this point in your life, there is no time like the present to make it better. As a cancer survivor, I know there is no guarantee of tomorrow. While we have time, why don't we all take a few moments to ask God to reveal what, if anything, we are lacking in our relationship with Him. It will be time well-spent.

Selah.

12

Timing is Everything

Often the outcome of a baseball game is determined by timing. Where do we see the value of timing on the baseball field? How about players who have a high percentage of hits when runners are in scoring position? This is a statistic that must drive managers crazy. A loss can be directly attributable to failing to get a hit when a runner is on second or third base. A player can get 3 hits out of 4 plate appearances, but if his one failure was the one and only at-bat when a runner was in scoring position, then his failure to get a hit could dramatically affect the outcome of the game.

How important is timing for a player who is stealing a base? If he leaves too soon, he gets picked off. If he leaves too late, he gets thrown out by the catcher. If he slides too early, he doesn't get to the base before the throw. If he slides too late, his momentum takes him past the base, and he is tagged out.

What about a fielder who has to dive or jump for a ball? We see this in its most dramatic fashion when an outfielder leaps and catches a ball that is over the fence. You can search YouTube for some of the more dramatic catches, but the catch by Austin Jackson, the center fielder for the Cleveland Indians, at Fenway Park on August 1, 2017, has to be one of the greatest catches ever made. He timed his jump perfectly to catch the ball, but his momentum caused him to hit and flip over the fence. He ended up in the Boston Red Sox bullpen, but he still had possession of the ball.

One of the most unnoticed acts of timing is when the manager puts in the right player at the right time that affects the outcome of the game. One of the most exciting walk-off home runs by a pinch hitter was in game one of the 1988 World Series between the Los Angeles Dodgers and the Oakland Athletics. Tommy Lasorda, the manager of the Dodgers, selected Kirk Gibson to pinch hit for Dave Anderson with two outs in the bottom of the ninth. The A's were winning 4 to 3 at this point, but the Dodgers had a runner on base. The count was 3 balls and 2 strikes when Dennis Eckersley threw his 7th pitch of the at-bat. Gibson hit the ball over the right field fence, and the Dodgers won the game 5 to 4.[55]

In case you are wondering, the major league record-holder for pinch hit home runs is Matt Stairs. He hit a total of 23 pinch hit home runs during his 19-year career. He is closely followed by Cliff Johnson (20), Jerry Lynch (18), and Gates Brown (16).[56]

****

Acts 17:26-27
Romans 8:28

As you look back over your life, have you ever wondered how timing has affected where you are today? Have you ever wondered why you were born in a certain place or in a particular century? How has timing affected the job, house, or spouse that you have? Some people seem to have perfect timing. They are always in the right place at the right time to get the opportunity they need to be successful. Matt Stairs was, at a minimum, in the right place at the right time when he hit 23 pinch-hit home runs in his career.

Others seem to have remarkably bad timing. But even the timing of difficult circumstances affects what decisions we make and ultimately, the path we take in life. Take John Walsh

---

[55] en.wikipedia.wiki/1988_World_Series
[56] baseball-almanac.com/recbooks/pinch-hitters-records.shtml

as an example. His television show, "America's Most Wanted," has probably done as much, if not more, to apprehend wanted criminals than any other law enforcement program in the U.S. What was Walsh's motivation for hosting the show? Possibly, it was the abduction and subsequent murder of his son, Adam Walsh, in 1981. He turned a horrible personal tragedy into something that has prevented crime and saved others from becoming a victim.

As we think about the timing of seminal events in our lives, another question comes to mind. Are these events purely random or is there a rational explanation as to why they occur when they do? Let's see what the Bible has to say on this subject.

On one of his missionary journeys, Paul arrived in Athens, Greece. In Acts 17, we read about a speech Paul gave at the Aeropagus after seeing an inscription on an altar that read, 'To an Unknown God.' As he was explaining who God is, Paul said in verses 26-27 that,

> "From one man he [God] made every nation of men, that they should inhabit the whole earth; and he [God] determined the times set for them and the exact places where they should live. God did this so that men would seek him and perhaps reach out for him and find him, though he is not far from each one of us."

These verses tell us that God has chosen when, where, and how long we should live, and that He did this so that we would seek and find Him. It is not an accident or coincidence that you are living in a specific location at this time in history. While it is true that mankind has free will and can choose where and how he or she will live, it is God's plan that wherever we are, we seek to know Him and do His will. To those who choose to serve God, the believer has another promise that can give you comfort when you do not understand why a time of difficulty comes your way.

In Romans 8:28, we read,

> "And we know that in all things God works for the good of those who love him who have been called according to his purpose."

We tend to focus on the first part of this verse and neglect the preconditions in the second part. This promise is reserved for "those who love him who have been called according to his purpose." If we love God and are striving to fulfill His purpose in our lives, then we have the assurance that God will work out the difficulties in our lives for good and not for bad.

As you think about your current situation in life, remember that God has determined the time and place where you will live. Ask yourself if you love Him and whether you have surrendered your free will to live out His purpose for your life. If you have, you are on solid ground, and you have the promise that God will work out your situation for good.

Let me encourage you to trust that God will direct you in the decisions you make, and He will work out the timing to meet your every need. We tend to get impatient, but God's timing is always perfect. Just like a manager who puts the right player in the game at the right time, God will place you in the center of His will if you ask.

Selah.

13

Stealing Home

One of the most exciting plays you will ever see in baseball is when a runner on third base steals home. It is a bold and risky decision on the part of the runner since he is already in scoring position. It is bold because it is rarely attempted. It is rarely attempted because it is extremely difficult to steal home without being thrown out. A runner has to find the perfect combination of surprise and inattentiveness to steal home successfully. For most players, it is safer to wait for a passed ball or for the batter to hit the ball before attempting to score.

The most recent occasion that I saw someone steal home was in a game on April 9, 2019, between the Boston Red Sox and the Toronto Blue Jays. Lourdes Gurriel, Jr., a Toronto Blue Jay, was on third base, and Chris Sale was pitching for the Red Sox. Rafael Devers, the third baseman for the Red Sox, was playing a good distance away from third base, and Chris Sale was pitching from his wind up instead of from the stretch. While Sale was focused on the signal from the catcher, Gurriel noticed that he was being ignored. Gurriel, Jr. broke for home, and he was easily called safe at the plate. It was a rewarding moment for Gurriel, Jr., and without a doubt, a disappointing one for the Red Sox.

Gurriel, Jr. is not the first player to successfully steal home. It has been done many times over the years, but it is still rare enough that it is exciting to watch. Ty Cobb is baseball's career leader in stealing home plate with 54.[57] He also holds the single-season record with 8 in 1912. Amazingly, there are 11 different players that have two stolen bases of home plate in

---

[57] baseball-almanac.com/recbooks/rb_stbah.shtml

a single game. A total of 53 players have at least 10 thefts of home plate in their careers. Some of the more notable names on that list include Honus Wagner (27), Jackie Robinson (19), Rod Carew (17), Lou Gehrig (15), and Babe Ruth and Paul Molitor who each had 10.[58] If there is one way to really help your team, it is to steal home when you get the opportunity.

****

Acts 4:19-20

Two of Jesus' disciples made a bold and daring move to 'steal home plate' in Acts 3. Peter and John were on their way to the temple at the time of prayer when they saw a man crippled from birth being carried to the temple gate. Peter and John looked at the man, and Peter commanded him in the name of Jesus to walk. Instantly, the man's feet and ankles became strong, and he walked. After the man was healed, Peter preached a message to the crowd, and Acts 4:4 tells us that about 5,000 men put their faith in Jesus.

This was a bold and risky move by Peter and John. What if they declared the cripple man to be healed, but he still could not walk? Peter and John would have been mocked and exposed as frauds. But the story does not end there.

In Acts 4, we read that the religious leaders had Peter and John arrested and put in jail. After the leaders questioned Peter and John about the healing and heard Peter's response, the leaders warned and threatened them to never again speak to anyone in the name of Jesus. What was Peter and John's response to these threats? Verses 19-20 give us the answer:

> "But Peter and John replied, 'Judge for yourselves whether it is right in God's sight to obey you rather than God. For we cannot help speaking about what we have seen and heard."

---

[58] Id.

Wow! This is a different Peter than the one who denied Jesus when he was confronted by a servant girl after Jesus' arrest. The Peter we see here was bold, courageous, and undeterred from his mission to spread the gospel.

As we live our lives, I wonder if we lack boldness and courage in certain areas. I am not speaking about being reckless, brash, or aggressive in our decision-making or conduct. The courage and boldness I'm speaking about is first and foremost grounded in love—love for God and others. Isn't this what we see in Peter and John? They were respectful to the leaders even though they arrested and threatened them. The healing of the crippled man, the message to the crowd, and the responses to the religious leaders were all motivated by love. We read nothing about Peter and John being angry or threatening revenge for being unlawfully imprisoned. We simply see two men who were bold and determined enough to risk, not only embarrassment, but their lives to share the good news about Jesus.

This discussion is not simply about raising the question of whether we lack boldness and courage to share the gospel. It is much broader than that. What risks, if any, do you need to take to create a better life for your family? Is it to seek another job or start your own business? Is it to step out of your comfort zone and volunteer in the community or at church? Or, is it to run for the local school board or city council to put you in a position to have a positive impact on the people in your community? It could be a myriad of situations where we need to ask ourselves and God if this is an area where we need to take a chance.

As you contemplate what God may be asking you to do, remember that we are not alone. God is with us and for us if we commit all our ways to Him and seek His guidance. Remember the love, courage, and boldness of Jesus. He left heaven to come to a sin-filled earth; He became flesh and blood and was subject to temptation and fatigue just like we are; and He was beaten, mocked, and crucified for a crime He did not commit so that we might have a relationship with God and attain eternal life.

Jesus stole home for us. It was a bold and daring move that changed the outcome of our lives. If we are like Him, our lives will be characterized by the same daring and boldness, and we too can better the lives of those around us.

Selah.

14

0 for 54

In 2016, Chris Davis, a first baseman for the Baltimore Orioles, signed a seven-year $161,000,000 contract.[59] According to the contract, his base salary will be $17,000,000 per year. Unfortunately for Davis and the Orioles, his performance has not risen like his salary. From 2016 through June 2019, Davis' batting average, home runs, and RBIs have decreased. In 2018, Davis played in 128 games, he had 470 at-bats, and his batting average was below the "Mendoza Line" at .168.[60]

The "Mendoza Line" is a baseball term that denotes a .200 batting average.[61] It is a general reference point or measuring stick that signals that a player needs additional hitting instruction. A player that falls below the "Mendoza Line" is in danger of being demoted to the minor leagues or possibly, being designated for assignment. "Designated for assignment" is a fancy term for what non-baseball players call being fired.

You may wonder why Davis garnered such a big salary if he is playing so poorly. The short answer is that Chris Davis has had tremendous success as a major league baseball player. In 2013, Davis hit 42 doubles and 53 home runs making him only the third player in history to hit more than 40 doubles and 50 home runs in a single season. The other two players who accomplished this feat were Babe Ruth in 1921 and Albert Belle in 1995. In 2013, Davis won the prestigious silver

---

[59] si.com/mlb/2019/04/13/baltimore-orioles-chris-davis-hitless-record-snapped
[60] baseball-reference.com/players/d/davisch02.shtml#all_br-salaries
[61] en.wikipedia.org/wiki/Mario_Mendoza

slugger award, and in 2015, he earned his second American League home run title.[62] Besides being a power hitter, Davis is also known for his outstanding fielding ability.

Despite having numerous accolades attached to his name, Davis has also earned an uncoveted distinction. From the end of the 2018 season through April 12, 2019, Davis was 0 for 54 at the plate. Every player goes through a slump, but no one, at least at this point in history, had ever gone that long without a hit. The previous hitless record-holder was Eugenio Velez who had gone 0 for 46. On April 13, 2019, Davis broke up his hitless streak by capturing 3 hits in a game against the Boston Red Sox at Fenway Park.[63] Even though the hitless streak is over, Davis has continued to struggle at the plate. As of this writing, he is still below the "Mendoza Line" with a batting average of .177.[64]

Time and again we hear interviews of players where they talk about "trusting the process" when they are going through a slump. I suspect what they mean by this is that their coaches have them performing certain drills to help them improve their hitting while all along knowing that improvement takes time. Their hope is that even though marked improvement may not happen overnight, one day it will come if they continue to follow their practice regimen.

****

Psalm 46:1
Matthew 11:28-30

To whom much is given, much is required. We read words to this effect in Luke 12:48. This scripture does not solely apply to our relationship with God. It has practical application in the secular world as well. Take Chris Davis' hitting slump for

---

[62] en.wikipedia.org/wiki/Chris_Davis_(baseball)
[63] Id.
[64] baseball-almanac.com/players/player.php?p=davisch02

example. The media attention his hitting slump has received would not be nearly as extensive if Davis was an average player with an average salary. The fans expect more from Davis because he is a great player with a huge salary. Because they expected more from him, no one knows better than Chris Davis the extra pressure he has felt to perform—pressure from others and from himself. As a Christian, do you feel the same kind of pressure to perform?

When a person becomes a Christian, he recognizes how much God has done by sending Jesus to die for his sins. His resurrection gives us hope of a future resurrection that will take us into the presence of God. Besides salvation, look at the other gifts God has given us. How about the privilege and right to be called a son or daughter of God with the full right of inheritance as His child? What about the gift of the Holy Spirit who teaches, corrects, strengthens, and comforts us in times of trouble? What about the gift of peace you feel knowing that God loves you and has forgiven you of your sins? And what about the other promises God gives the believer that are in the Bible? To say a Christian has been given much is a gross understatement.

Knowing we have all these wonderful gifts from God, how do we feel when life becomes hectic and difficult? You know what hectic and difficult looks like. It is when you have done everything your boss has told you to do, but he remains dissatisfied with your work to the point that your job is in jeopardy. It is when you have spent years raising your kids right, but they rebel and can't stand being around you. Or, it is when you pray your heart out for an urgent need, and it feels like your prayers hit the ceiling and are never heard by God.

In those times, do we feel like we are in a "slump?" Do we feel like that if we just pray harder, volunteer more often, or spend an extra hour reading the Bible that life will miraculously return to normal? In those times, do we tend to press too much to the point that we become difficult to be around? What we tend to forget is that just like a batter has a process for getting out of a slump, God may want us to be patient and trust Him as we go through the process of discovering what we need to learn and how God will deliver us from our difficulty.

During times of difficulty, most of us probably look for a cause of the problem. We may conclude that the cause is attributable to us, someone else, an uncontrollable circumstance, or some combination of all of the above. But there is another option.

Not every difficult period in our lives is due to a misstep on our part. Sometimes it is due for reasons unknown to us. Let's use Daniel as an example. In Daniel 10, Daniel had seen a terrifying vision of the future, and he was left feeling helpless, with no strength, and he was deathly pale. When an angel appeared to Daniel 21 days later, the angel explained to Daniel that his prayer to understand the meaning of the vision was immediately heard by God, but the angel was detained by the prince of Persia (a demon) who was attempting to prevent the angel from reaching Daniel with the interpretation he sought. You can read this in Daniel 10:4-14. Daniel's answer to prayer was slow in coming not because Daniel had sin in his life, but because, unbeknownst to Daniel, there was a spiritual battle taking place in heaven.

Like Daniel, Job had a similar experience. Job had done everything right in God's sight, and yet, God allowed Satan to test Job with the loss of his children, his health, and all his possessions (Job 1-2). In the end, God reminded Job that God was sovereign over everything, and Job was fully restored.

Where do we go and what do we do when life stinks and we feel like a failure? Do we go to work, the golf course, or the liquor cabinet to get away from it all? Do we complain about our problems to whoever will listen, or do we hold it inside until one day we explode? None of these options seem to be very helpful, do they?

When we are in doubt about what to do to solve a problem, wouldn't it be helpful to look in the Bible to see what God says? I will refer to two passages. In Psalm 46:1, the psalmist says,

> "God is our refuge and strength, an ever-present help in times of trouble."

Let those words sink in.

The psalmist is stating a truth, but he is also making a statement of faith. The Bible tells us what the truth is, but it is up to us, with God's help, to believe that truth and act on it. If we truly believe God is our refuge and strength, and He is always present to help us when trouble arises, then we have nothing to fear. We may not be immediately delivered from the problem, but He will help us through it. Remember Daniel and Job. Each was delivered, but neither was delivered from their suffering immediately.

In Matthew 11:28-30, Jesus stated,

> "Come to me, all you who are weary and burdened, and I will give you rest. Take my yoke upon you and learn from me, for I am gentle and humble in heart, and you will find rest for your souls. For my yoke is easy and my burden is light."

It is tiring and burdensome when we feel like we have failed our children, our employers, our church, or whoever we have let down. The good news here is that Jesus invites us to come to Him, and He will give us the rest we need.

The word "yoke" is not a word we hear or use very often in our conversations so let's look at the definition. "Yoke" is primarily defined as "a wooden bar or frame by which two draft animals (such as oxen) are joined at the heads or necks for working together."[65] This definition may have been what Jesus intended by "yoke." Jesus' hearers would have been familiar with the term since seeing oxen yoked together to plow a field was common in Jesus' day.

I don't profess to know everything about what Jesus meant when He referenced His "yoke," but it suggests to me that for us to live in God's will, it takes a joint effort. First, God will do His part by keeping His promises. There are too many promises to name all of them here, but the Bible is full of them. One promise He has made is to raise up the believer at the end of the world to meet Jesus in the air so that we can be with God forever. (1 Thessalonians 4:16-17).

Second, we must do our part. This is where the baseball analogy of how a batter gets through his slump is instructive. Do you remember when it was mentioned that the player has to "trust the process?" He has to trust his hitting drills will one day help him consistently hit again. Without that trust, he has no hope. When hope is lost, his baseball career is over.

It is the same with us. Our job is to trust the process. When we experience trouble in life, or we feel like we have let down our family, our employer, our church, or our community, we need help. Instead of going to God for help, we try to fix it ourselves. By doing so, we put on the yoke that God intended to carry—the yoke of achieving results. Isn't it our place to trust God and obey His word? Isn't it God's job to achieve the result He intends? Too many times we burden ourselves with something we were never intended to carry. Faith is our responsibility. The results are His.

---

[65] dictionary.com/browse/yoke?s=t

For example, you can share your faith in Jesus with your son or daughter, but if they do not believe, are you to blame? You can lovingly raise your kids to be honest and law-abiding citizens, but if they break the law, is that your fault? No. It may be tempting to blame yourself, but that may be an example of you taking on the yoke of being responsible for the results in the life of your child.

The burden that Jesus wants us to give to Him is the burden we carry to achieve results. Baseball is a performance-based business. You perform to achieve the desired result, or you lose your job. Our relationship with God is different. While we have a duty to obey, our relationship with God is largely based on grace. We follow Him and leave the results to God. If today you are burdened, weary, and feeling like a failure, find rest in the fact that Jesus wants to carry that burden for you. Trust the process of walking by faith and leave the results to God.

Selah.

15

Is Time Running Out?

Some of the most popular sporting contests in the U.S. are controlled by a clock. Football has four quarters that are timed, and each play must begin within a specific number of seconds or the offense is penalized. Basketball, hockey, and soccer all have time clocks as well. There are a few sports that do not utilize a time clock. One of those is baseball.

The absence of a time clock has been a blessing and a curse for baseball. The blessing falls on the players. Mainly, it gives the pitcher and batter time to ready themselves before a pitch is thrown. It also allows a team to continue to play until there is a winner when the score is tied after a nine-inning regulation game is completed. Theoretically, a baseball game could continue indefinitely if the score remains tied after the completion of each inning. Baseball games can last several hours, but fortunately, none of them have continued indefinitely. The longest extra innings game was on May 8, 1984 between the Chicago Cubs and the Milwaukee Brewers. It lasted 8 hours and 6 minutes. The shortest nine-inning game ever played was on September 28, 1919 between New York and Philadelphia. It lasted only 51 minutes.[66]

The curse of not having a time clock falls on the fans because boredom sets in when a game drags on for hours. We tend to forget that baseball is part of the entertainment industry. If a game goes on and on with seemingly no end to it, people lose interest. Fans may want to spend a few hours at the ballpark, but the slow pace of play has become a real issue in

---

[66] baseball-almanac.com/recbooks/rb_gmig.shtml

professional baseball. The thinking is that if the speed of the game is not increased, then fans will lose interest and no longer want to pay money to see a game. The fear is that fans will find another form of entertainment that is not as time-consuming as baseball.

Negotiations between the MLB owners and the players' union have brought up the idea of implementing a pitch clock to increase the pace of play, an idea that is not popular with the players. Instead of forcing the issue, the MLB decided to implement two new rules for the 2019 season. The first limited the number of mound visits, and the second implemented an intentional walk rule that no longer requires a pitcher to throw 4 pitches to walk a batter.[67] As for the pitch clock issue, we will have to wait and see if it is implemented in the 2020 season.

****

2 Corinthians 6:1-2
James 4:13-14

Many things in our lives are controlled by the clock. We fight rush hour traffic to get to work. We rush breakfast for the kids so they can get to school on time. We hurry to the airport because the plane will leave at a specific time with or without us. We even battle against the calendar, not just the clock. We have to be conscious about the time limit we have to renew our car registration, pay our taxes, or make an Airbnb reservation. The list goes on and on. The clock can control our lives if we are not careful.

On the other hand, the clock has at least one positive attribute. It sets a deadline for us to act. You may not have this problem, but some people tend to procrastinate and never

---

67

content.mlb.com/documents/2/2/4/305750224/2019_Official_Base ball_Rules_FINAL_.pdf seem to get anything done. You remember those book reports in high school. How many of us waited until the night before to start working on them? The same thing happens in college. How many students wait until the night before to cram for a final? It even seems to happen in baseball. How many times have you watched a game where it seems like your team doesn't start scoring runs until the 8th inning? In hindsight, it seems ridiculous to waste so much time before we finally do what we should have done days, weeks, or innings ago. Procrastination, in those circumstances, only serves to put more pressure on us.

In other circumstances, the effect can have more severe consequences. I can think of at least two instances where procrastination caused a person's family members to suffer a significant financial loss. One involved a man who failed to have a will executed before his death, and the other involved a failure to make an election upon retirement that caused the surviving spouse to lose thousands of dollars. I'm sure you can think of other examples where people believed they had plenty of time to act, but time was not on their side and others paid for their mistake.

I wonder if there is a "clock" in our relationship with God. If there is a "clock," do we know how much time we have left before we can make things right with God or reconcile with others? Can you imagine what it would be like to play a sport with a game clock such as football and the players do not know how much time is left before the game ends? What would be the effect of having time tick away without knowing how much time is left? Wouldn't it create a sense of urgency to score as quickly and as often as possible to avoid losing the game?

In 2 Corinthians 6:1-2, we read,

> "As God fellow workers, we urge you not to receive God's grace in vain. For he says, 'In the time of my

favor I heard you, and in the day of salvation I helped you.' I tell you, now is the time of God's favor, now is the day of salvation."

There is no guarantee of tomorrow. In fact, there is no guarantee of another hour, minute, or second. We get lulled into a false sense of security and forget this truth until the sudden death of someone close to us reminds us that life is short. Paul appears to be telling the Corinthians that instead of wasting the time that God has graciously given them, they should choose today to accept God's offer of salvation. For some people, it is a temptation and a trap to think that they can live the way they want to while they are young and accept the gospel later in life.

The apostle James, who was Jesus' half-brother, states it this way in James 4:13-14:

"Now listen, you who say, 'Today or tomorrow we will go to this or that city, spend a year there, carry on business and make money.' Why you do not even know what will happen tomorrow. What is your life? You are a mist that appears for a little while and then vanishes."

We may presume tomorrow will come, but we cannot guarantee it will come for us. James' description of our lives as a mist is a vivid picture of how temporary our lives really are. If people took the time to consider the enormous risk they take by putting off the decision to accept the gospel, they would realize it is not a gamble worth taking. The problem may, in part, be due to the fact that we have trouble grasping the height and depth of what it means to be eternally separated from God.

Unlike baseball, there is a time clock running down in life, and no one knows how much time is left before time runs out. In order to live with no regrets, shouldn't we have a sense of urgency and take the opportunity today to reconcile our relationship with God and those around us? If you have doubts about your relationship with God, then ask Him to show you what you need to do to have the peace you are looking for. If you are estranged from a family member or friend, ask God to show you how you can restore that relationship. As you search your heart, remember God is in the reconciliation business. Isn't that why He sent His Son in the first place?

Selah.

16

Mound Visits

The higher salaries in professional baseball are traditionally reserved for pitchers. Why is that? Without good pitching, it is extremely hard to consistently win. If you pay attention to the transactions that take place near the trade deadline, you will notice that the teams most likely to be in the playoffs are always trying to improve their pitching. Good hitting wins games, but good pitching wins championships. While some may disagree, pitchers are paid more than other players because they are absolutely vital to a team's success.

The official rules of baseball direct that the pitcher's mound should be a circle with an 18-foot diameter. The pitcher's plate, commonly referred to as the rubber, must be a rectangular slab of white rubber, 24 inches by 6 inches. Rule 2.04 requires the distance from the rear point of home plate to the pitcher's plate to be 60 feet, 6 inches. Rule 2.01 states that the pitcher's plate shall be 10 inches above the level of home plate. The rules further dictate the slope of the mound and require that the degree of the slope be uniform.[68]

The mound is the pitcher's domain, and for the most part, it is the focal point of the game. This is because play does not begin until a pitcher throws the ball. When a pitcher is doing well, you will rarely see anyone approach the mound to talk to the pitcher. But when a problem arises, there can be a crowd on the mound.

---

[68]

content.mlb.com/documents/2/2/4/305750224/2019_Official_Base ball_Rules_FINAL_.pdf

What kind of problem requires a mound visit? It could be an injury to the pitcher, a miscommunication between the catcher and the pitcher, a need to discuss the best pitch to throw to a batter in a high-leverage situation where there are men on the bases, the pitcher's mechanics are askew and causing him to have trouble throwing strikes, or to make a pitching change.

Oftentimes, only the catcher will approach the pitcher's mound to discuss something with the pitcher. Other times, the pitching coach and the infielders will discuss something with the pitcher. Usually, when the manager comes to the mound, the pitcher knows he is being replaced, and his day is over.

Mound visits are an important part of the game. They can avoid a miscommunication between the catcher and pitcher, help the team execute their strategy against a particular batter, correct a mechanical error in the pitcher's throwing motion, or encourage the pitcher to persevere to get the next out. But the number of mound visits have lengthened baseball games to the point that it required an amendment to the official rules. Rule 5.10(m) now limits the number of mound visits to five per team, per nine innings. A pitcher can receive the guidance, correction, and encouragement he needs, but teams now have to be more efficient in how they use their mound visits.

****
2 Timothy 3:16-17
Romans 12:6-8

Each of us lives, works, and plays among people in a particular geographic location, and whether we realize it or not, each of us has influence over the people we interact with on a daily basis. A pitcher's domain and his primary area of influence is the pitcher's mound. What he does or does not do in that 18-foot circle, for the most part, affects the outcome of the game. So, it is with each of us.

Our family, co-workers, church, and community depend on us to be our very best. What we say and how we conduct ourselves can affect the attitude, financial condition, health, and emotions of those who interact with us. When we are at our best, we may not need a "mound visit" to receive correction or encouragement. But how often are we at our best? We may have more days when we are not at our best than days when we are. In those trying times, we need to lean on the advice and encouragement of others to help us return to the path that God is leading us down.

If we are honest, all of us have times where we need correction in how we are living or thinking. It may not be something major, but if it is not corrected now, it could turn into something serious later. Take church attendance for example. A pattern of coming to church two times per month can turn into coming once every two months and so on. Before you know it, you haven't been to church in a year, and your relationship with God is practically nonexistent. Some people may not think they get anything out of going to church, but what they fail to realize is that other people may need them to be there to give others the encouragement and support they need.

In those times where we are "off our game," where do we go and from whom do we get the advice and encouragement we need? I am glad you asked. One source of help is the Bible. In 2 Timothy 3:16-17, Paul stated,

> "All Scripture is God-breathed and is useful for teaching, rebuking, correcting and training in righteousness, so that the man of God may be thoroughly equipped for every good work."

God has given us the Bible to use as our compass in life and as a means to help us understand who He is and how He wants us to live. Consider for a moment where we would be if the

Bible did not exist. There would be no absolute truths to live by and each person would decide in his own heart what was right and what was wrong. Frankly, it would be a disaster if we did not have the Bible.

The second source of help I want to focus on is the help we receive from other people. Have you ever considered how dependent we are on others? Some people sincerely believe they are self-sufficient, and don't need any help. Are they correct, or sincerely wrong?

Let's take clothing as an example. We buy clothing at a store and fail to consider that someone had to grow the cotton or make the material to be used to manufacture the clothing. We overlook that someone had to buy the clothing from the manufacturer and then build a store to offer it for sale. Finally, they set a price and agree to sell it to us, the consumers. This shortened version of the process of how clothing comes into our possession is only one example of how dependent we are on each other. In truth, isn't it a bit short-sighted to think that we can live without the help of others?

Who do I need advice and help from when I "can't throw a strike?" A doctor, counselor, pastor, spouse, best friend, trusted co-worker, or relative to name a few. Anyone who is wise and truly cares about you is a good place to start. Paul reminds us in the Book of Romans that God has given certain gifts to believers that are designed to edify or build up the church. In Romans 12:6-8, we read,

> "We have different gifts, according to the grace given us. If a man's gift is prophesying, let him use it in proportion to his faith. If it is serving, let him serve; if it is teaching, let him teach; if it is encouraging, let him encourage; if it is contributing to the needs of others, let him give generously; if it is leadership, let him

govern diligently; if it is showing mercy, let him do it cheerfully."

There are two sides to this coin. First, sometimes we need help, and we should not be too proud to ask for it. God has put people in our lives that can help us if we will just look for them. Second, we may be the one that someone needs to go to their "mound" and give them a word of encouragement. It is nice to be helped, but true joy comes when we help someone else. In Paul's farewell to the Ephesians, he reminded them that Jesus once said, 'It is more blessed to give than to receive.' (Acts 20:35). How true are those words?

What are you struggling with? Do you seem a little "off" in your attitude or in how you treat people? Has complacency and procrastination kept you from doing what you know you should do? All of us struggle from time to time, but the wise person recognizes it or has someone who will lovingly help him identify what is wrong. A pitcher has his coach and teammates to help him make an adjustment. The believer has the Holy Spirit, the Bible, and other Christians to help him continue in the will of God. Be encouraged to seek help when you need it and be willing to help others when they can't seem to "throw a strike."

Selah.

17

Baseball is More Than a Game

On April 25, 1976, the Los Angeles Dodgers were hosting a game against the Chicago Cubs. In the bottom of the fourth inning, two protesters ran onto the field carrying the U.S. flag and a lighter. The protesters stopped in center field, unfurled the flag, and doused the flag with lighter fluid. The first match they lit was blown out by the wind. Before the second match lit the saturated flag, Rick Monday, the centerfielder for the Chicago Cubs, swooped down on the unsuspecting protesters, grabbed the flag, and ran away with the flag undamaged. In the top of the fifth inning when Monday came to bat, the Dodger fans gave him a standing ovation for his act of patriotism in saving the flag.[69]

Monday played 19 seasons in the MLB, the last 8 of which was with the Los Angeles Dodgers. He was a two-time All-Star, and he was a member of the 1981 Los Angeles Dodgers when they won the World Series. Over his career, he hit 241 home runs, he had 775 RBIs, and his batting average was .264.[70] Even though he had a remarkable baseball career, Monday will probably be best remembered for saving the flag in Dodger stadium over 43 years ago.

Where is the flag today? Monday still has it. In fact, it is reported that he has been offered $1 million dollars for the flag, but he has refused to sell.[71] Instead, it has been reported that Monday and his wife take that same flag around the

---

[69] foxnews.com/sports/on-this-date-cubs-outfielder-rick-monday-saved-an-american-flag-from-protesters
[70] baseball-almanac.com/players/player.php?p=mondari01
[71] en.wikipedia.org/wiki/Rick_Monday

country to raise money for military charities.[72] What others intended to do with the flag to protest against war, Monday has turned into good by raising money to help the soldiers who protect our freedom.

****

Philippians 3:7-11

As we consider what Rick Monday did 43 years ago, have you wondered why he risked his safety to prevent the protestors from making a political statement? After all, Monday's baseball responsibilities did not require him to run toward the protestors and rescue the flag. Well, only Rick Monday can say why at that moment he did what he did, but it must have been obvious to the fans that Monday did not appreciate someone disrespecting the country he loves. Why else would he turn down a $1 million dollar offer and instead, use the flag to raise money for military charities unless he loved America and appreciated the sacrifice that our soldiers make to preserve our freedoms? Because of his heroics 43 years ago, Rick Monday may be remembered more for his love for America than any baseball statistic attached to his name. In this one event, we see the intersection of Monday's love for baseball and our country, and love for country won out.

If you have been a Christian for any length of time, it has probably been ingrained in you that it is important to pray, read your Bible, go to church, tithe, and volunteer in your church and community. All of these practices are vital, and if you are already doing these things, you are to be commended. But how often do you think we do what is expected, and yet, fail to reflect on why we do them? Is there more to being a Christian than just reading your Bible, praying, and going to church? Have we forgotten our first love?

---

[72] mlb.com/news/rick-monday-saving-american-flag-resonates/c-174266502

These questions concerning our relationship with God can easily be redirected to our relationships with our spouses, children, co-workers, and fellow congregants. Would you agree that something is missing in your relationship with your spouse if you simply go through the motions of being kind, respectful, fiscally responsible, and obedient? That doesn't quite sound like the marriage you envisioned when you said, "I do," does it?

What about your relationship with others? Are those relationships limited and superficial because you have not taken the time and made the effort to make them special? Are we going the "extra mile" to nurture those relationships, or are we doing only the bare minimum to maintain them?

As we consider these questions, it would be helpful to take a moment to reflect on Paul's relationship with Jesus Christ. It will prove to be helpful because Paul's relationship with Jesus shows us what our relationship with God and others should look like.

Paul was a person who was committed to his calling, and he was the type of person who believed no sacrifice was too high to fulfill that calling. In today's vernacular, Paul was "all in" with everything he did. It makes no difference whether you consider his life prior to believing in Jesus or after he made his profession of faith. We see the same Paul—driven, dedicated, sincere, determined, and almost unstoppable. If you need a reminder of some of Paul's accomplishments and sufferings for Jesus, you can read about them in 2 Corinthians 11:21-29. Speaking for myself, Paul's accomplishments and commitment to excellence in all of his relationships make mine look pretty lame.

Let's take a few minutes to look a little deeper at Paul's relationship with Jesus. Paul reveals his heart to us in Philippians 3: 7-11:

"But whatever was to my profit I now consider loss for the sake of Christ. What is more, I consider everything a loss compared to the surpassing greatness of knowing Christ Jesus my Lord, for whose sake I have lost all things. I consider them rubbish, that I may gain Christ and be found in him, not having a righteousness of my own that comes from the law, but that which is through faith in Christ— the righteousness that comes from God and is by faith. I want to know Christ and the power of his resurrection and the fellowship of sharing in his sufferings, becoming like him in his death, and so, somehow, to attain to the resurrection from the dead."

There is great wealth in these 5 verses, and honestly, more than I can fully comprehend. Instead of dissecting every phrase, let's hit the high points.

First, Paul cherished knowing and having a relationship with Jesus more than anything in this world. Second, he considered his earthly accomplishments as nothing when compared to his great love for Christ. Third, he knew his relationship with Jesus was not based on his exemplary compliance with the law, but on faith in what Jesus did for him on the cross. Fourth, he was willing to pay the ultimate price, namely, death, to know Jesus and become like Him. If there ever was a picture of what an intense, passionate love for Jesus Christ looks like, this is it.

God wants each of us to have that kind of relationship with Him. Isn't our love for God the reason we pray, read our Bible, go to church, tithe, and serve in the church and community? If it isn't, then shouldn't it be? What about your relationship with your spouse? Don't you do the things you do out of love for your spouse? If it isn't out of love, then shouldn't it be? Finally, what about your relationships with your children and others? Shouldn't those relationships also be based on a genuine love for them? It is easy to get distracted by the cares of life and forget what is truly important. Our relationships are the most important thing we have in life. If we nurture them and go beyond what is expected to make them better, our lives will be more fulfilling than we could have ever imagined.

In 1976, Rick Monday went beyond what was expected of him as a baseball player, and it changed his life forever. He will always be remembered for his patriotism and saving the flag. The apostle Paul sacrificed everything to know Christ and to make him known, and he will be greatly rewarded for his intense love for God and others. What about us? What do we want God to remember us for? How do we want our family and others to remember us? Will they remember us as someone who did only what was needed to get by, or as someone who made the extra effort to have a deep, personal, and lasting relationship with them?

Selah.

18

The Closer

A closer in baseball is a relief pitcher that usually enters the game in the final inning to help his team hold onto their lead and win the game. The closer is often thought of as the team's best relief pitcher, and depending on the circumstances, his job is to get the last 3 outs of the game. If he is successful, he does not get credit for the win, but he is credited with a save. If he is unsuccessful, he is considered to have blown a save opportunity. Being a closer is a high-pressure job because the victory is in jeopardy when he enters the game. In short, the closer is either the hero or the villain. He is the face of victory or the image of defeat. It is all or nothing.

Why do teams need a closer? Why don't the starting pitchers finish the game they started? Aren't we taught to finish what we started and never quit until the job is finished? Those are all good questions that deserve an answer. The answers lie more in strategy than in giving up.

If you research the all-time career complete game leaders, you will find that the top 18 were all born in the 1800s. Warren Spahn, who is 19th on the list, was born in 1921, and he is credited with 382 complete games.[73] Spahn played in 1942 and again from 1946 through 1965, his career being interrupted by World War II. It appears that most pitchers in the early days of baseball pitched the entire game or at least, more frequently than they do today. It wasn't until 1924 that we see pitchers consistently having double-digit saves in a

---

[73] baseball-almanac.com/pitching/picomg1.shtml

season. The first such pitcher was Frederick "Firpo" Marberry who had 15 saves in 1924 and 1925 and 22 saves in 1926.[74]

As we fast-forward to today, we usually see multiple relief pitchers for each team in a nine-inning game. The strategy today seems to be to have the starter pitch six innings and have 3 relief pitchers who throw 95+ mph pitch one inning each to finish the game. The thinking is that by using several pitchers, it puts more pressure on the batters because they are facing a pitcher with a fresh arm and one they have not seen before in the game. But there is another reason why most starters don't finish the game. They get tired, they can't throw a strike, or both. Sometimes the best pitcher needs help. That help comes from the "relief pitcher."

By the way, who is the all-time career saves leader? If you answered "Mariano Rivera," you are correct. He had 652. He is closely followed by Trevor Hoffman who had 601 career saves.[75]

****

John 15:12-13
Psalm 121:1-2

We know that in our jobs, relationships, health, and even our daily routine we encounter problems we did not expect. Let's consider a few practical examples. You get a flat tire on the way home from work, and when you look for the tire tool to loosen the nuts, you remember you left it in the garage. You think the relationship you have with your son is in good shape, but you find out he has been mocking you on social media. You have been doing a good job at work, but your boss comes into your office and tells you that you are being let go because of budget cuts. You get the picture.

---

[74] baseball-almanac.com/pitching/pisave4.shtml
[75] baseball-almanac.com/pitching/pisave1.shtml

Life is not always like baseball. In life, we can't "leave the game" and expect someone else to finish the job we started like a reliever does for the starting pitcher. No one can live our lives for us. We alone must finish what God has called us to do, but that does not mean we have to do it alone.

It is like a patient who has had hip replacement surgery. To get stronger, he must go to physical therapy. The physical therapist cannot do the exercises the patient must do, but the therapist can encourage, instruct, and help the patient reach his goal. A batting coach cannot go to the plate and hit for the player. Only the player can do that. But the coach can encourage, instruct, and help the player get out of his slump.

As believers, do we desire to do the will of God? Do we share the same conviction that Jesus had when He said His food was to do the will of God and to finish his work (John 4:34)? Do we long to say, like Paul, that we have fought the good fight, finished the race, and kept the faith (2 Timothy 4:7)? I believe we do, but the truth is we need help to finish our race, and we need to help others do the same. There are two scriptures that will be helpful as we strive to do the will of God and as we seek to help others persevere in what God has called them to do.

In Psalm 121:1-2, the psalmist states,

> "I lift up my eyes to the hills—where does my help come from? My help comes from the Lord, the Maker of heaven and earth."

Looking up into the sky, as if to peer into heaven itself, is a common posture for people when they are thankful or when they are in desperate need. Without hearing a word, their posture tells the onlooker they are looking to God for help or giving Him thanks. Committing these verses to memory would probably serve us well for two reasons. First, it is a confession that we cannot be the person God wants us to be in our own strength. Second, it tells God that we know our only hope for help is found in Him.

The second scripture is found in John 15:12-13. Jesus stated,

> "My command is this: Love each other as I have loved you. Greater love has no one than this, that he lay down his life for his friends."

Do these verses remind you of why you help others with their problems? The "why" of what we do is sometimes referred to as our motive. Jesus' motive for laying down His life and dying for our sins was His tremendous love for us. Doesn't Jesus remind us here that He is our standard, and we should love each other as He loves us? It is oftentimes hard, inconvenient, and time-consuming to help those around us, but have you considered how we could change the world if we, and others, simply obeyed verses 12 and 13? Just like a closer who gets the final out, loving others the way Jesus loves us would be a game-changer. It would change the world.

Before we finish this discussion, it would be prudent for all of us to ask ourselves if we are operating in our own strength or looking to God each day for His help and guidance. It would also be wise for us to consider who we come in contact with on a regular basis that could use a word of encouragement. In a world full of anger, hate, and disrespect, a kind word of encouragement can go a long way in helping us fulfill the great commission by reaching the lost.

Selah.

19

From Player to Manager

We can only speculate how long and hard the road is for a player to make it to the major leagues. For the elite players, the road is short and relatively easy. There have only been 21 players who were drafted and immediately went to the major leagues. The last player to do so was Mike Leake in 2010.[76] For others, the road from the minors to the majors is long and hard. For example, John Lindsey was drafted 347th in the 1995 draft, but he did not make his MLB debut with the Los Angeles Dodgers until 2010.[77] He faithfully toiled in the minors for 15 years before he finally made his first appearance in the major leagues.

How long is a MLB career? It varies, but for argument's sake, let's say a player retires at 35 years of age. Now that he has retired, what is his next career? One profession that some players have pursued is the logical step of becoming a manager. If you think about it, who is in a better position to know the game than the players who have spent their lives studying baseball and striving to become the best players they can be? Once their physical skills dwindle, some players realize they can still use the knowledge they gained over their careers to teach and manage younger players.

Over the years, there have been several players who became major league managers after having retired as a player. A few of the more well-known are Frank Robinson, Joe Torre, Joe Girardi, Mike Scioscia, Paul Molitor, Kevin Cash (current

---

[76] baseball-almanac.com/feats/feats9.shtml
[77] baseball-almanac.com/players/player.php?p=lindsjo01

manager of the Tampa Rays), Dave Roberts (current manager of the Los Angeles Dodgers), and Aaron Boone (current manager of the New York Yankees).

There have also been a few players who took the extraordinary step of being a player-manager. This is a person who performs both functions simultaneously. He is a current player who is also the manager of the team. There have been approximately 222 player-managers in MLB history. This number is only a little over 1% of all players who have played in the major leagues. The last American league player-manager was Don Kessinger (Chicago White Sox) in 1979, and the last National league player-manager was Pete Rose (Cincinnati Reds) from 1984-1986.[78]

A baseball manager performs many different functions. He oversees fielding and batting practice, juggles the different personalities on the team as he makes up the line-up for each game, answers questions from the media, makes game decisions such as when to insert a relief pitcher or pinch hitter, has discussions with the team's general manager about player personnel, and of course, spends an enormous amount of time traveling with the team.

The manager is the leader, encourager, teacher, communicator, and overseer of the team as a whole and the individual players who make up the team. One important quality of any good manager is that he must be a person who can relate to and have a personal relationship with his players. That personal relationship is critical because without it the players will be less likely to accept instruction, correction, or discipline when that becomes necessary.

****

Proverbs 27:17

---

[78] baseball-almanac.com/managers/player-managers.shtml

The role of the manager, and in particular, the player-manager is illustrative of what some of our relationships should look like as we mature. The reason the player-manager analogy is more suitable is because each of us has more to learn in life and in our relationship with God. No matter how old we are or how vast our life experiences have been, there is still more to learn. But doesn't there come a point in life that we can share what we have learned with those around us who are younger and have less experience? You guessed it. The subject for consideration in this chapter is mentoring.

In the past, when I considered the idea of mentoring, I immediately thought that was someone else's job. Mentoring was better suited for someone else, so I believed, because I had enough trouble keeping myself straight much less helping someone else deal with the stresses of life. Today, I have a different perspective on mentoring that may prove helpful for us to consider.

Proverbs 27:17 states,

"As iron sharpens iron, so one man sharpens another."

The general background for this verse centers on the practice of rubbing two iron blades against each other to sharpen and make them both more effective. The thought goes that people can sharpen and make each other more effective by having contact with and learning from one another. When there is contact, there is usually friction. Friction can be good, for example, when it keeps your car tires on the road, but it can also be harmful if it irritates an already tenuous relationship. Since there is a potential for harm, it is vital that a mentoring relationship be based on a solid foundation.

One definition of a "mentor" is "a wise and trusted counselor or teacher."[79] If we use this definition and I consider you to be my mentor, then, by definition, I consider you to be not only my counselor and teacher, but someone I believe is wise and trustworthy. What would you have to do before someone saw you with these attributes?

For one thing, it would take time—time to demonstrate those qualities to the person or at least, time to build that reputation. It would also require special knowledge and the ability to apply that knowledge by making good decisions. Finally, you would have to have a personal relationship based on trust with the person you are mentoring before they would consider you to be trustworthy. In short, it would require you to unselfishly give up your time to teach, encourage, and counsel someone with much less experience to help them succeed.

How many little league and high school baseball players do you think could have played in college or even the MLB if they would have had someone to mentor them on an individual basis? How many lawyers, plumbers, doctors, etc. would have avoided grievances and complaints if they would have had a mentor to help them be better at their jobs? How many Christians would have saved their marriages, raised their children to love God, or been a more effective communicator of the gospel if they would have had someone to mentor them in those areas?

As in all things, why don't we look to Jesus to see if He was a mentor, and if so, how He went about it? Jesus had a limited time on earth, and it is commonly believed that He spent only 3 years in public ministry. As savior to a world that did not recognize Him as such, He lived a life where He fulfilled prophecy, worked miracles, preached of His coming to save

---

[79] dictionary.com/browse/mentor?s=t

the world from its sins, and mentored 12 men to continue His work after His death and resurrection. More to the truth, He successfully mentored only 11 men who would continue to spread the gospel since Judas Iscariot committed suicide after betraying Him.

Jesus was the perfect mentor. He was wise, trustworthy, humble, loving, patient, unselfish, knowledgeable, experienced, and spoke with an authority the people had never seen or heard before. He was the consummate leader. How did He mentor His disciples? First, He basically lived with them for three years. This was probably necessary since Jesus knew His time was short. I am not suggesting here that for us to mentor someone we should make ourselves their houseguest. The point here is that Jesus spent countless hours with His disciples instilling in them the truth about God and Himself. He even told them things He knew they would not understand until after His death and resurrection. He planted the seed that would only grow after they received the Counselor, the gift of the Holy Spirit.

Second, He selected the 12 men who would be known as His disciples. The Bible does not describe what Jesus was looking for in a disciple, but it is safe to say that Jesus saw qualities in them that would one day cause Jesus to entrust them with the gospel of salvation. Jesus had a close, personal relationship with each of His disciples, and they knew He had a deep abiding love for them.

Third, Jesus not only taught them with His words, but He demonstrated what it looked like to live a holy and godly life. There was no hypocrisy in Jesus because His private and public lives were the same. In fact, His life of godliness and holiness was so impeccable the religious leaders had difficulty finding any evidence that would justify crucifying Him (Mark 14:55-59).

If you listen carefully to the interviews of MLB players, on occasion, you will hear a player express gratitude to another player for taking the time to teach him about the intricacies of the game. A rookie in the MLB has a lot to learn, and he learns much more quickly if another player helps him along his journey. It is the same way in life. You and I may not measure up to be the mentor that Jesus was, but we can follow His example and ask God to use us to help someone else. If we don't feel qualified to be mentors, we can find help in the same statement of faith Paul made in Philippians 4:13 when he said, "I can do all things through Christ who strengthens me."

Who do you know that could use a mentor? Do you have the type of relationship with that person that would allow the person to accept your help and words of wisdom? Do you have the personal attributes that would make you a good mentor? Consider being a mentor to someone. I am grateful for the different people in my life who have guided, encouraged, taught, and corrected me in my walk as a believer. I am sure you are also. How about we return the favor and speak life into someone who has just started their journey of faith?

Selah.

20

Baseball, a Family Affair

Have you ever noticed MLB players with the same last name? Did you wonder if they were related? With a little research, I learned that there are 394 brother combinations that have played in the major leagues.[80] Out of those 394, there have been approximately 105 brother combinations where the brothers played on the same team. Some of the more recognizable brothers include Billy and Cal Ripken, Jr. (Baltimore Orioles); Pedro and Ramon Martinez (Los Angeles Dodgers and Boston Red Sox); Tony and Chris Gwynn (San Diego Padres); Hank and Tommie Aaron (Atlanta Braves); and Roberto and Sandy Alomar, Jr. (San Diego Padres, Cleveland Indians and Chicago White Sox).[81]

There have been approximately 237 father-son combinations in the major leagues, but there have only been two father-son combinations that were teammates.[82] They were Ken Griffey and Ken Griffey, Jr. (1990-1991 Seattle Mariners) and Tim Raines and Tim Raines, Jr. (2001 Baltimore Orioles).[83] Out of those 237 father-son combinations, 12 fathers and two sons became Hall of Famers. The two sons were Ken Griffey, Jr. and Roberto Alomar.[84]

We can all probably agree that it is extremely difficult to get to the major leagues. How about this? What is the likelihood that brothers in the same family will be professional players?

---

[80] baseball-almanac.com/family/fam1.shtml
[81] baseball-almanac.com/family/fam6.shtml
[82] baseball-almanac.com/family/fam2.shtml
[83] baseball-almanac.com/family/fam6.shtml
[84] baseball-almanac.com/family/fam2.shtml

After you consider that, what is the likelihood the brothers will be on the same team? How about the chances that you and your father are major league players and you end up as teammates? The odds of that happening must be astronomical. A person well-versed in probability theory would be like a kid in a candy store trying to calculate the likelihood of that happening.

On the other hand, it should not surprise you when you learn about family members making their livelihood in the same profession. They have the same genes, same upbringing, and the same love for baseball. They may not play the same position, have the same skill level, or make similar salaries, but they are still family members striving to be the best baseball players they can be.

****

Matthew 12:47-50
Galatians 3:26-28

What would it be like if every believer in Jesus Christ viewed every other believer as a member of his or her family? Before we answer that question, we should first consider whether the Bible teaches us that believers are part of a family. Two scripture verses will help us find the answer.

In Matthew 12: 47-50, we read,

> "Someone told him [Jesus], 'Your mother and brothers are standing outside, wanting to speak to you.' He replied to him, 'Who is my mother, and who are my brothers?' Pointing to his disciples, he said, 'Here are my mother and my brothers. For whoever does the will of my Father in heaven is my brother and sister and mother."

Jesus wasn't confused about the composition of his nuclear family. He had at least 4 step-brothers and 2 step-sisters. We know this from Mark 6:3. If Jesus wasn't confused, then what is He saying? Before we try to answer that question, let's look at what Paul said in Galatians 3:26-28:

> "You are all sons of God through faith in Christ Jesus, for all of you who were baptized into Christ have clothed yourselves with Christ. There is neither Jew nor Greek, slave or free, male nor female, for you are all one in Christ Jesus."

Can we deduce from these two passages that the people who put their faith in Jesus Christ and seek to do His will are sons and daughters of God? If, for example, my next-door neighbor has put her faith in Jesus and is a daughter of God, then in God's sight, aren't we part of the same family if I too have put my faith in Jesus? She is a daughter and I am a son, and we have the same father. Doesn't that sound like family to you? It does to me.

Notice what the criteria is for being part of God's family. The only requirements are that the person put his faith in Jesus Christ and seek to do God's will. That's it. Notice what is *not* the criteria. It does not require that believers hold the same beliefs on collateral issues. It does not require that all believers attend the same church or belong to the same denomination.

Moreover, it does not require all believers to be of the same gender, race, ethnic background, or position in society. In fact, doesn't the passage in Galatians suggest that when God looks at believers, He sees no differences whatsoever? He only sees believers as "one in Christ."

Let's pause for a moment and let that sink in.

Can you imagine how society would be transformed if we really believed this truth? Can you see believers of one denomination being kinder, more supportive, and in unity with believers from another denomination? Can you picture different churches and denominations working together in unity to fulfill the great commission of sharing the gospel and making disciples of all nations? Do you think believers would be more apt to treat each other as equals? If we truly saw each other as family members, would we promptly come to the aid or defense of other believers when we hear they are suffering, being criticized, or in trouble? How would this way of thinking affect our response when we hear about believers being persecuted around the world? The possibilities are almost endless.

Earlier I mentioned that it is not all that surprising that we see family members in professional baseball. They have the same genetic material, upbringing, and love for baseball. But isn't that even more true of believers? We have the same Father; we have the same blood that washes away our sins; we have the same Word of God that teaches us how to live; and we have the same love for God and desire to do His will.

As a believer in Christ, we should never feel abandoned or like an orphan. Our parents may be deceased and we may not have any blood relatives, but because we are believers, we are part of the family of God. We share an unbreakable bond with other believers that we may not share with our biological family members. That unbreakable bond is Jesus Christ.

Selah.

21

Law of Expectations

Our expectations explain why we react the way we do. If your expectations are low because your favorite team usually finishes last in the standings, then you are not angry when they lose. It was expected. On the other hand, if your expectations are high because your team has a history of winning, then you may be furious when they lose. You expected a better performance from your team so you became angry and disgruntled. The reverse is also true.

When you expect your team to lose, but to your surprise, they win, you are elated. When you expect your team to win and they do, your reaction is more subdued because you expected them to win. Our expectations determine our reaction. It is almost a mathematical formula. Expectations + Result = Our Reaction. This principle applies in every aspect of life, but we are here to talk about baseball for now.

How do the salaries of particular baseball players affect what you expect from them on the field? Would you agree that the higher paid players are expected to perform at a higher level than the lower paid players? How do you feel when the highest-paid player on your favorite team is in a slump or can't seem to throw a strike? Do you find yourself getting more frustrated or angry at him than you do with a player that may also be performing poorly but is not being paid as much? If you feel this way, you have experienced the law of expectations.

Who were some of the highest-paid players in the MLB in 2019? The top 10 highest-paid players and their salaries for 2019 were as follows:

1. Stephen Strasburg -- $38,333,333
2. Max Scherzer -- 37,400,000
3. Zack Greinke -- $34,500,000
4. Mike Trout -- $34,100,000
5. David Price -- $31,000,000
6. Clayton Kershaw -- $31,000,000
7. Miguel Cabrera -- $30,000,000
8. Yoenis Cespedes -- $29,000,000
9. Justin Verlander -- $28,000,000
10. Albert Pujols -- $28,000,000[85]

As you can see, the elite players make more money in one year than most of us could ever hope to make in a lifetime. But along with the high salary comes high expectations. A failure to perform at a level that matches the expectation will produce a negative reaction from the fans, and if it continues, it will result in a reduction in pay when it is time to sign a new contract.

There is another variable that affects our expectations that has not been mentioned. That variable is the possibility that our expectations are unrealistic or based on a lack of information. Do you expect more from others than you do from yourself? If so, then possibly your expectations are unrealistic. How many times have we become frustrated with the performance of a player only to find out later that he had an injury we did not know about? If we had known about the injury, our expectations and resulting frustration would probably have been much lower.

****

---

[85] mlb.com/news/highest-paid-players-in-2019

Luke 12:48b
Luke 9:23-25

What do we expect from God?

As mentioned earlier, the law of expectations extends to every area of life, not just baseball. Do you expect and demand more from your children than from your neighbor's children? Do you expect more from your spouse and your friends than you do from a stranger? We can all probably answer "yes" to both of these questions. There is nothing wrong with expecting more from people that we love, have a special relationship with, or have provided for financially. In those relationships, we justifiably feel that we have given them much, and therefore, much more is required from them than from someone we do not know. Does the Bible support this premise?

In Luke 12:48b, we read,

> "For everyone to whom much is given, from him much will be required; and to whom much has been committed, of him they will ask the more." (NKJV).

This verse comes toward the end of a parable that Jesus was using to explain that the punishment for those who knowingly fail to obey God will be more severe compared to the punishment received by those who unknowingly fail to obey. To the one, God has entrusted a more thorough understanding of who He is and what He requires that the other does not have. To the one who has been given much, much is required. To the other who has been given less, less is required.

It is because of this principle in Luke 12:48 that some people deceive themselves into thinking that if they do not read the Bible, then they won't be held as accountable for its contents than those who read it daily. Their thought process is that if they are ignorant of the truths in the Bible, then they have not been given much, and therefore, much will not be required of them. Does that sound like a strategy that will trick God into holding them less accountable?

There is one glaring problem with this thought process, and it has to do with access to the word of God. Isn't it reasonable to hold someone who has ready access to the Bible more accountable for its contents than someone who has no access? Do we really think that just because someone who has access to, but refuses to read, the Bible will be held less responsible for its contents than someone who has never heard there is a Bible?

There may also be another problem that arises when people refuse to make a sincere effort to know God by reading the Bible. Because they do not know God and His character traits, they have unrealistic or incorrect expectations of Him. For instance, people who see God as a God who is eagerly waiting to punish each misstep a person makes tend to blame Him when things don't go well. They see it as God punishing them, but the Bible teaches the exact opposite. God not only loves us, He is love. (1 John 4:8). Love is an integral part of His character. Their conclusion that God is punishing them stems from a misguided expectation that punishment is what God seeks to do. Therefore, they get angry at God for something He never did.

As we consider the question of what we expect from God, it may be wise to first consider whether our expectations are unrealistic or based on a lack of information. What better way is there to develop an accurate concept of who God is and what He is like than to read and study the Bible? If we neglect to do that, do we risk having a distorted view of God and His character?

If we have access to God's word and fail to read it, we miss a golden opportunity to know Him. Moreover, we will not avoid being held responsible for our ignorance about God and His will. A failure to read the Bible is like receiving a love letter from your spouse and ignoring it. You miss out on discovering what is in your spouse's heart, and, at the same time, you risk offending your spouse if you refuse to read his or her letter. You lose twice. Is that how God feels when we neglect spending time with Him?

There are several things that we expect from God. They are so numerous, in fact, that only a few will be mentioned here to make the point. We expect God to:

1. Be true to His word;
2. Love us unconditionally;
3. Be faithful in all things;
4. Be omnipotent, omnipresent, and omniscient;
5. Grant our prayer requests;
6. Work a miracle for us when we need one;
7. Raise us from the dead so we can live in heaven with Him; and
8. Save our family members.

How does this list look to you? Do you have a right to expect all of these from God or only some of them? Are all 8 absolute truths we can count on 100% of the time or are some of them conditional on what we or others do? Take a minute to consider your answer before we go any further.

It appears that items one through four are absolute truths we can rely on all the time. Those items are essential parts of God's character, and He, unlike us, never changes. As for the remaining items, whether God does those things depends upon whether it is His will and whether we ask for them in faith. How many of us are thankful that God has not answered our every prayer request the way we wanted it to be answered?

God will raise us from the dead and save our family members if each of us repents of our sins and asks Jesus to be Lord and Savior of our lives. Even though God wants to save our family members, each of them must pray for and seek that salvation for themselves. God has given each person a free will to choose or not choose Him. He will not override that right of choice.

What does God expect from us?

The answer to this question is only found in the Bible because that is, for the most part, where we learn what God expects from us. What does the Bible say? God expects us to:

- Love Him with all our being and make Him our number one priority in life (Luke 10:27; 14:26);
- Love our neighbor as we love ourselves (Luke 10:27);
- Pray with faith (James 1:5-8);
- Live by faith (2 Corinthians 5:7);
- Accept Jesus as our Lord and Savior (John 3:16);
- Help the poor (1 John 3:17);
- Pray for and submit to those in authority (1 Timothy 2:1-2; Romans 13:1);
- Deny ourselves, take up our cross, and follow Jesus (Luke 9:23-25);
- Be patient until Jesus returns (James 5:7); and
- Do justice, love kindness, and walk humbly with God (Micah 6:8).

Again, the list is too long to comprehensively mention in this book all that God expects from us. As you read the Bible, you can add to my list.

What God expects from us may raise additional questions.

- Does God have the right to expect all these from us?
- Do we have the ability to do what He expects?

- What if we fail to live up to His expectations?
- Have we been given much from God that now justifies God demanding much from us in return?

I will leave the first three questions for you to answer as you read the Bible and seek Him in prayer. As to whether we have been given much, we can see God's blessings and goodness in all aspects of our lives. Just the fact that we can breathe is evidence of God's goodness. As we count all the blessings God has bestowed upon us, isn't He more than justified in asking that we give him our lives and all that we have?

We demand much from the elite players in baseball because they make enormous sums of money. They have been given much so we expect much from them. God sent His only Son to die for our sins so that we can have a relationship with Him. Wouldn't you agree that we have been given much? Moreover, wouldn't you agree that the little we have to give to God is nothing compared to what He has given us? Surely, we can give our lives, as lowly as they may be, to the God of all creation.

Selah.

22

It Takes Teamwork

On May 8, 2019, the Boston Red Sox defeated the Baltimore Orioles in 12 innings by a score of 2 to 1. The victory exemplified how important teamwork is to win a baseball game. Mookie Betts homered early in the game. Chris Sale pitched 8 strong innings with 14 strikeouts. Eduardo Nunez knocked down a grounder while playing second base that not only kept the ball from going into the outfield, but at the same time, prevented the runner on third base from scoring the winning run. Jackie Bradley made a home run-saving catch on a ball hit by Trey Mancini that would have won the game for the Orioles. Andrew Benintendi hit a home run in the 12th inning that put Boston ahead for good.

Every win and every loss in baseball is due to teamwork. In a victory, we tend to focus on one or two players that performed exceptionally well, such as the player who pitched a shutout or the one who hit the game-winning home run. In a loss, we are quick to point a finger at the player who made an error or struck out with the bases loaded as the reason why the team was defeated. Our opinion of the team, at least on that day, is derived from the performance of one or two players, whether good or bad, to the exclusion of the rest of the team. But regardless of the result, there are other players that were an integral part of the game. They may be marginalized by the fans or media, but the team recognizes the role each player made for that day's result.

To have teamwork, you first must have a common goal. In baseball, the goals are clear—win the game, win your division, and win the World Series. But one thing can negatively impact the teamwork that is necessary to win, and that is an absence of unity. A game played on September 27, 2015 may serve as a good example.

In a game between the Washington Nationals and the Philadelphia Phillies, Bryce Harper made an out and as he entered the dugout, he was met by one of his teammates, Jonathan Papelbon. The two exchanged words, and Papelbon could be seen grabbing Harper by the neck and pushing him against the wall of the dugout. The two had to be separated by their teammates. The Nationals ended up losing the game by a score of 12 to 5.[86] While there may have been other reasons for the loss, it is safe to say that the altercation between two players on the same team did not help them in their pursuit of victory.

****

Matthew 12:25
1 Corinthians 12:24b-27

Sharing a common goal and using unity and teamwork to achieve the goal sounds simple enough, but what may be simple in theory can be more complicated in reality. How are these concepts related?

Are teamwork and unity hard to achieve if the goal is not clearly defined? What if we too narrowly define our primary goal and fail to state our secondary goals? For example, the primary goal of most businesses is to make money, but what about a secondary goal of having high employee morale? If the business is so focused on the primary goal of making money, how long will it continue to function if it neglects the morale of its employees? What happens if the goal is viewed as too lofty or unattainable by the team? Will that promote or discourage a unified effort to achieve the goal?

---

[86] mlb.com/news/jonathan-papelbon-bryce-harper-altercation/c-151946476

Let's consider these questions with the global Church in mind. If you were asked what is the goal of the Church, what would you say? Some might say it is to preach the gospel to all nations. Others may say it is to worship God, preach the gospel, disciple those who accept the gospel, obey the commands in the Bible, and remain diligent until Jesus returns. But others may have a different view. What is your opinion regarding why the Church exists?

If we do not agree on something as basic as the primary purpose or goal of the Church, could that explain, in part, why there are so many Bible-believing churches? In Matthew 12, Jesus healed a demon-possessed man who was blind and mute. When the religious leaders claimed Jesus' power came from the prince of demons, Jesus stated,

> "Every kingdom divided against itself will be ruined, and every city or household divided against itself will not stand."

Division causes ruin. It is no respecter of size. It can reduce to ashes something as large as a kingdom or as small as a household. The greatest threat to a family, business, church, city, state, or nation is not from outside forces, but from within. There are several factors that can cause division in a church, but let's only talk about one for now. What about the feeling that some church members have that they are not needed or unqualified to advance the church's mission?

You may be thinking that someone who feels this way may not participate in the activities of the church, but they can hardly be described as divisive. You may be technically correct, but if people feel this way, then their absence or lack of effort causes the church as a whole to be less effective in fulfilling its mission. A baseball example and a scripture verse may be helpful.

In 2019, a team in the MLB was allowed to carry 25 players during the regular season. It is common for teams to have approximately 13 pitchers on a team, leaving 12 players to play the field. Since there are 8 position players on the field beside the pitcher, this only leaves a few extra position players to substitute for injuries or as a pinch hitter. If the team has 13 pitchers and 5 of those are starters, then that leaves 8 relief pitchers. If one of those relief pitchers feels like he isn't needed since there are several relief pitchers for the manager to put in the game, he may not prepare for that day's game as he should. What happens when the manager puts in a relief pitcher who isn't prepared to pitch? Disaster.

Some of you may see this example as fairly unrealistic for at least two reasons. First, how could anyone on a MLB team feel they were not needed or unimportant since becoming a major league player, by itself, is a considerable achievement? Second, the simple fact that the roster is limited to 25 players means that these players are the best the organization has to win baseball games.

Those of you who feel this way are exactly correct. Each player is crucial to the success of the team especially in games where a player is injured or the game goes into extra innings. How is it, though, that we can clearly see the importance of each baseball player, regardless of their position, but we fail to see the importance of each believer in the life of the church?

In 1 Corinthians 12:12-31, the apostle Paul compares the function of the church to the human body. In verses 24b-27, he stated,

> "But God has combined the members of the body and has given greater honor to the parts that lacked it, so that there should be no division in the body, but that its parts should have equal concern for each other. If one part suffers, every part suffers with it; if one part is

honored, every part rejoices with it. Now you are the body of Christ, and each one of you is a part of it."

Is Paul's point here that each believer is an important part of the body of Christ (the Church) even though each person has different qualifications and functions? Is he emphasizing that if one member of the church chooses not to exercise his or her gift in the ministry of the church, then the whole church suffers? Is he reassuring his readers that together they make up the body of Christ and each individual is an essential part of that body?

It is easy to see the gifts and talents in others, but we fail to recognize what God has given each of us to help the Church fulfill its mission. It may even, at times, seem like the mission of the Church to reach the world with the gospel and make disciples of all nations is an unattainable goal. Despite how we feel, we may be underestimating the power of God to achieve His will through people like you and me. God wants every person to have a saving knowledge of Him, and He wants us to help someone else have that same relationship.

What gifts or talents has God given you to help the church? Do you realize how important you are to the local church in helping it fulfill its mission in your community and to the world? Isn't it true that more often than not, the most important functions of the local church are those that are less visible than the more prominent ones? Like the parable of the talents, God will reward us with more if we are faithful with what He has given us (Matthew 25:14-30). Give God your best. You will never regret it.

Selah.

23

Keep Your Eyes on the Ball

In theory, hitting a baseball is simple. Keep your eye on the baseball, swing only at strikes, and let the balls go by. In practice, hitting is not as simple as it sounds. If there was one proven formula for consistently hitting a baseball, you would not see the variety of batting stances that are displayed on a baseball field. The position of the feet, hands, hips, and bat vary from player to player. Some players have an open stance while others have a closed stance. Some players stand erect while others crouch at the knees. Some players hold the bat perpendicular to the ground, others hold it parallel to the ground, and still others somewhere in between. The styles of hitting are as unique as the personalities of the players.

But there are aspects of each swing that players have in common. With each swing, there is a shifting of the player's weight from his back leg to his front leg. The hands remain back while the player's hips rotate forward with the shift of his momentum. Most importantly, the player's eyes are fixed on the baseball as the bat makes contact with the ball. In fact, the player's eyes should never leave the baseball from the point the ball leaves the pitcher's hand until the ball crosses the plate or strikes the player's bat.

Keeping your eyes on the ball is impui tant for several reasons. First, it is hard to hit what you cannot see. Second, it is vital that the batter see the rotation of the ball as it leaves the pitcher's hand to help the batter identify the type of pitch being thrown. Since a batter has only a fraction of a second to decide whether to swing at a pitch, it is important to get a good look at it as soon as possible. Third, observing the movement on the ball will help the batter decide whether it will be a strike, a ball, or a pitch that is about to hit him. Fourth, hitting is the essence of winning. The axiom that 'if you can hit, you will play' is true. The reverse is equally true. If you can't hit, you won't play.

Bad things usually happen when a batter takes his eyes off the baseball—he swings at a pitch that is not a strike; misses the pitch; hits a foul ball; or makes weak contact with the ball resulting in an out. You may be wondering what can cause a batter to take his eyes off the ball? There are many specific reasons, but one general explanation encompasses them all—distractions. The distraction may be due to what the batter sees behind the pitcher. If the background blends in with the color of the baseball, then it is much harder for the batter to see the pitch and hit it.

It may be due to not being mentally sharp at the plate. If the batter's mind is not entirely focused on watching the ball, he will be distracted and not make good contact with the ball. We know there are times when we are distracted at work, and our minds begin to wander. Baseball players are human just like us. There is no reason to think they are somehow exempt from being distracted simply because they are being paid to play baseball.

Finally, it could be the distractions present in the ballpark itself. The people in the crowd, the noise, or the player wondering about the ability of the home plate umpire to accurately call balls and strikes.

What baseball player would you say was the least distracted at the plate? In other words, who do you consider to be the best hitter in MLB history? Was it Babe Ruth who had 714 career home runs and a career batting average of .342?[87] Was

---

[87] baseball-almanac.com/players/player.php?=ruthba01

it Ty Cobb who had 4,189 career hits and who is the career batting average leader at .366?[88] Would it be Hank Aaron who had 755 home runs, 3,771 career hits, and a career batting average of .305?[89] Or, would it be someone else like Pete Rose, Ted Williams, Joe DiMaggio, Stan Musial, or Derek Jeter?

****

Hebrews 12:2-3

Colossians 3:1-2

What is the equivalent of 'keeping your eyes on the ball' for you personally? Does it mean your focus is on:

- keeping your job so you can support your family?
- becoming a more patient person?
- faithfully praying and reading your Bible on a daily basis?
- obeying God's word, and discerning His will for your life?

The concept of 'keeping your eyes on the ball' is more urgent and crucial for a Christian than it is for a baseball player. But what constitutes 'keeping your eyes on the ball' for each believer is comparable to batting stances. There are several differences, some similarities. Each person, at any given point in time, has a unique set of issues he or she is dealing with. Those issues can be linked to his or her finances, physical health, marriage, emotional condition, children, church, or anything else that comes up in life. How those issues are resolved are as varied as the problems themselves.

On the other hand, every believer shares a common path with other believers that leads to rest and peace of mind when the problems of this life tend to overwhelm us. It is the path that

---

[88] baseball-almanac.com/players/player.php?=cobbty01
[89] baseball-almanac.com/players/player.php?=aaronha01

helps us 'keep our eyes on the ball.' In Hebrews 12, the author states in verses 2-3,

> "Let us fix our eyes on Jesus, the author and perfecter of our faith, who for the joy set before him endured the cross, scorning its shame, and sat down at the right hand of God. Consider him who endured such opposition from sinful men, so that you will not grow weary and lose heart."

The problems of this life can cause us to feel anxious, fearful, angry, tired, and despondent. But if we fix our remembrance on what Jesus endured for us to perfect our faith, don't the struggles on earth become 'light and momentary' to use Paul's words in 2 Corinthians 4:17? Have you ever really taken a moment to consider what Jesus had to endure on the cross?

Besides the horrendous physical trauma, He was mocked, humiliated, and ridiculed in a public place for everyone to see and hear. The problems you and I deal with are serious, but are they anything compared to what Jesus endured for us while we were still sinners?

In Paul's letter to the Colossians, he directs us to another avenue that leads to peace and rest and will help us live above our circumstances. In Colossians 3:1-2, Paul states,

> "Since, then, you have been raised with Christ, set your hearts on things above, where Christ is seated at the right hand of God. Set your minds on things above, not earthly things."

This verse does not teach us to be so heavenly minded that we are no earthly good, but instead, it encourages us to keep our focus on God and not the troubles in this life.

Have you ever set your mind and heart on something? At that time, how would you describe yourself? Would you say you were undeterred, focused, and relentless in your pursuit of what you desired? If we can be that focused on an earthly pursuit, can we have that same intensity in our relationship with God? Isn't that the way God wants our relationship with Him to look like?

What would it look like to be so focused on spiritual things and our relationship with God that the burdens of this life seemed light and momentary? I am not talking about shirking our responsibilities at work, home, church, or in other areas. What these verses in Hebrews and Colossians remind us is that if we want to live an undistracted life for God, we must keep our eyes, mind, and heart focused on Jesus Christ.

Is your life full of distractions right now? Do you feel tired and worn out? Have you taken your eyes off what is truly important and become drained by the cares of this life?

If you answered "yes" to any of these questions, you are not alone. God's word is not designed to curb our enjoyment in life, but to enhance it. His word sets boundaries and guides us for our protection. The Bible gives us the solution when we allow the troubles of this world to weigh us down. Like hitting, the solution is simple. Instead of swinging only at strikes and letting the balls go by, the believer takes his or her eyes off the problem and puts them on the problem-solver. His name is Jesus.

Selah.

24

Signs and Signals

Communication is an essential part of winning. Put another way, a failure to communicate can make the difference between winning and losing a baseball game. How often have we seen outfielders fail to communicate with each other when a routine fly ball is hit that results in the two players colliding and the ball falling to the ground? Have you seen plays where a catcher is expecting a breaking ball, but the pitcher throws a fastball that gets past the catcher and allows the runner on third base to score? There are innumerable games that could have had a more desirable ending if the players would have communicated effectively.

Where do we see signs and signals on the baseball field, and what is their purpose? The first place we see signs is between the catcher and pitcher. These signs are usually conveyed from the catcher by covertly using a certain number of fingers to suggest to the pitcher what should be the next pitch. The pitcher nods or shakes his head to signal to the catcher that he will or will not throw that pitch.

Why don't they just verbally shout out what the pitch will be instead of all this finger-pointing and head shaking? You know why. If they publicly announce what the pitch will be, it makes it much easier for the batter to hit the pitch. This would promote effective communication between the pitcher and catcher, but it prepares the batter for the next pitch.

Why don't they dispense with the signs and let the pitcher just throw the pitch he wants to throw without informing the catcher beforehand what the pitch will be? If that happened, the catcher would be at a greater risk of injury, or he might fail to catch the ball. A failure to catch the ball is not concerning if the bases are empty, but if there is a player on base, the runner could advance to another base or score a run. This method of pitching is not a viable option because it puts the catcher in an untenable position to safely catch the ball.

Finally, what happens if the pitcher misconstrues the sign given by the catcher and he throws a pitch the catcher did not expect? We have the same possibilities in the previous example—an injury or a passed ball.

The second place we see signs or signals is from the third base coach to the batter and/or a player that is on base. To a spectator that is unfamiliar with baseball, the third base coach may appear to be swatting flies or suffering from a nervous disorder when he goes through a series of gestures to signal to the batter or runner what he wants them to do. A good example of this would be when there is a runner on first base, and the coach wants to put on a hit and run play. To successfully do this, the batter knows he must hit the next pitch because the runner will be running to second base as the ball leaves the pitcher's hand. This is a play that is designed to help the runner get to second base and at the same time avoid a double play.

If there is a miscommunication and either the batter or the runner fails to recognize the signal, then there is usually a bad result. If the batter is at fault by failing to swing at the pitch, then the runner will probably be thrown out at second. If the runner fails to run like he is supposed to, then there is a greater likelihood that a double play will occur. Again, these signals are given secretly so the other team will not know in advance what the offense intends to do.

The third place we see signs or signals is when the third base coach signals a runner who is approaching third base to either stop at third or run to home plate. This sign is not given secretly, but a failure to see the signal or obey it can be disastrous. It doesn't happen often, but there are occasions where a player sees but disregards the coach's signal to stop at third only to be thrown out at home plate. Guess who gets an earful in those situations? What is particularly frustrating about a play like that is the third base coach is clearly in the best position to see if the defensive player has the ball and is likely to throw the runner out at home, but the runner ignores that signal thinking he knows more than the coach.

There are a few other areas where signs or signals are used, but you get the point. Although the form of communication is different, it is vital that players effectively communicate with each other and their coaches to win a game.

****

2 Timothy 3:1-5
2 Peter 3:1-13

How important is communication in life? Put another way, what are the consequences if there is a failure to communicate? What happens when you and your spouse fail to communicate about which one of you will pick up your children after school? What happens when you missed the phone message at work from your boss that your deadline is earlier than you thought? What would happen if there was a failure to communicate that a hurricane or tornado was fast-approaching your city? It only takes a few examples to see the serious consequences associated with miscommunication to convince us how important it is to effectively communicate with each other.

The tech industry knows the importance of communication more than anyone. The number and type of computer programs and apps that facilitate communication between people who do or do not know each other is growing every day. The technical advancements that make it easier to communicate with others have in some cases made society better, and in others, it has made society worse. Despite the good or bad consequences, one thing is clear. People have a penchant for and a need to communicate.

How important would you say communication is in your relationship with God? If we neglect to communicate with God, would the results be the same as they would be if, let's say, you neglected to communicate with your spouse? What would happen if we did all the talking to God and never listened? Would the results be the same if we talked to our spouse, but never listened to what he or she had to say?

When the subject comes up about communicating with God, do you automatically think about presenting requests to God in the form of prayers? If so, you are not alone. Have you ever wondered when we pray how much time we spend talking compared to the time we spend listening? Is 99% talking and 1% listening about right?

As we consider the subject of communicating with God, do you think He wants to say something to us? If He does, but we fail to listen, how do you think that makes Him feel? Do you think He feels the same way we feel when people refuse to listen to us?

How do we listen to God? It is probably no different than what you do when you listen to another person. You get in their presence, and you use your eyes, ears, and brain to understand what the person is saying to you. We communicate with others by text, letter, voice, body language, phone, or email to name a few. We use our eyes, ears, and brain to understand what is being communicated. Can we all agree that God is not likely to send you a text, call your phone number, or send you an email? There have been examples of

God speaking audibly to people, but those are extremely rare. What about by letter? Is God still communicating to us by letter?

God still speaks to us through His written word, and at times, He refers to signs or signals of what is to come. There are several places in the Bible where God speaks of signs or signals of His coming or the end of time, but only two places will be mentioned here. God has been kind enough to forewarn us of certain events so we can be prepared to deal with them. As you read your Bible, look for other passages that you can share with those who are unaware of what God intends to do.

In 2 Timothy 3:1-5, Paul states:

> "But mark this: There will be terrible times in the last days. People will be lovers of themselves, lovers of money, boastful, proud, abusive, disobedient to their parents, ungrateful, unholy, without love, unforgiving, slanderous, without self-control, brutal, not lovers of the good, treacherous, rash, conceited, lovers of pleasure rather than lovers of God—having a form of godliness but denying its power. Have nothing to do with them."

Do we see any evidence that the last days are upon us? God wants everyone to be saved, and He wants us to love others and share the gospel with them. But, here, He also warns us to not get too close to the people described here. Could it be for our protection?

In 2 Peter 3:10-13, Peter states:

> "But the day of the Lord will come like a thief. The heavens will disappear with a roar; the elements will be destroyed by fire, and the earth and everything in it will be laid bare. Since everything will be destroyed in this way, what kind of people ought you to be? You ought

to live holy and godly lives as you look forward to the day of God and speed its coming. That day will bring about the destruction of the heavens by fire, and the elements will melt in the heat. But in keeping with his promise we are looking forward to a new heaven and a new earth, the home of righteousness."

While God tells us in advance how the earth will be destroyed, there are two more important points here. First, it will come suddenly and unexpectedly like a thief in the night. God wants us to know, for ourselves and for those we tell, there will be no time to be reconciled to Him before this event takes place. It will occur in the blink of an eye. Putting off our relationship with God is not a wise option. Second, this passage tells us what our reaction should be to knowing how the world will end. We should live holy and godly lives as we await His return.

These are just two passages that God has included in the Bible that provide us with the signs we should look for while we wait for His coming. Would you agree that one way we can listen to God is by reading the Bible to "hear" what He is telling us? A successful relationship depends on giving (talking) and receiving (listening) information. God can speak to us through other people, audibly, or in other ways, but He primarily speaks to us through the Bible.

If we fail to read the Bible, we run the risk of missing the signs and signals He is giving us to help us live an abundant life. We don't want to miss the stop sign at third base and get thrown out at home. In baseball, there is always another game with an opportunity to score. In life, there may not be.

Selah.

25

Recognizing an MLB Player

If you saw a MLB player at the grocery store, would you recognize him? Unless you closely follow baseball or the player's face is well-known from television commercials, the chances are good that you would not. What if the player was wearing his team uniform in the grocery store? Other than being slightly weird, it would probably help, but it may not be conclusive proof to help you identify him as a MLB player. The icing on the cake would be if you saw the player in his team uniform in the setting where he should be, namely, the baseball park. All three (the player, the team uniform, the baseball park setting) would convince you that the player was who you thought he was.

Millions of dollars are probably spent by fans each year on MLB merchandise. Fans buy hats, jerseys, shirts, batting helmets, and jackets of their favorite teams or players. By doing so, they are identifying themselves with those teams or players. Does wearing the paraphernalia make them a MLB player? No. What if they wear the merchandise at the ballpark? Would they be mistaken as a player? Probably not. But would all three—the physical conditioning of the person, the type of merchandise he was wearing, and what he was doing at the ballpark—be enough to convince you that the person you saw was or was not a professional baseball player?

****
John 13:35
1 John 4:20-21
Colossians 3:12-14

In a criminal case, the government has the burden of proof. It must prove the guilt of the accused beyond a reasonable doubt. If the proof does not exclude reasonable doubt, then the accused is found not guilty.

Have we ever thought that if we were accused of being Christians, would there be sufficient evidence to prove beyond a reasonable doubt that we were guilty as charged? What evidence could we point to that proves we are Christians? If we wear a cross around our necks and have an ichthys (fish symbol) magnet on our cars, would that be enough evidence? Surely, if we have the cross, the magnet, and attend church occasionally that would be enough evidence, wouldn't it?

We know that becoming a Christian begins with an internal belief that is then publicly professed, both verbally and in how we live our lives. Behavior follows belief. If we believe in Jesus Christ as our Savior and Lord, then our behavior will reflect that. So, what will that behavior look like?

In John 13:35, Jesus stated,

> "By this all men will know that you are my disciples, if you love one another."

Jesus seems to give us a litmus test here to prove to others that we are true followers of Christ—loving one another. Notice that Jesus did not narrow his idea of "another" to only those we like or that treat us in a loving manner. Let's investigate the context of Jesus' words.

He spoke these words at the last supper that He had with His disciples shortly before His betrayal by Judas Iscariot and His arrest. It also appears from verse 30 that Judas Iscariot was absent when Jesus spoke these words.

From the context, does the verse mean that Jesus only intended for His disciples, then and now, to love other like-minded disciples? In other words, is it our love for other Christians that will tell the world that we are Jesus' disciples? Or, is that love to be demonstrated to Christians and non-christians alike? John, one of Jesus' closest disciples, can help us here.

In 1 John 4:20-21, we read,

> "If anyone says, 'I love God,' yet hates his brother, he is a liar. For anyone who does not love his brother, whom he has seen, cannot love God, whom he has not seen. And he has given us this command: Whoever loves God must also love his brother."

John does not sugar-coat what is required for people to love God. If we love God, we must also love people. John clearly tells us that we cannot love God unless we also love our neighbor. If we are looking for proof of our Christianity, then we must reflect on whether we love and demonstrate love to those we encounter in our daily lives.

And if we need a refresher on what love looks like, then we can read 1 Corinthians 13:4-7 to remind us. Try personalizing verses 4-7 by inserting your name everywhere the word "love" appears. Why don't we all do that before we move on? When you put your name in verses 4-7, how closely did that describe you?

It was previously mentioned in this chapter about fans wearing baseball merchandise to identify with and publicly profess their allegiance to a particular team or player. The Bible also tells believers what to wear to publicly profess their allegiance to Jesus. In Colossians 3:12-14, we read,

"Therefore, as God's chosen people, holy and dearly loved, clothe yourselves with compassion, kindness, humility, gentleness, and patience. Bear with each other and forgive whatever grievances you may have against one another. Forgive as the Lord forgave you. And over all these virtues put on love, which binds them all together in perfect unity."

If we are looking for further evidence that we are true disciples of Christ, then maybe we should ask ourselves if verses 12-14 describe us. How would your world change if these verses perfectly described you? How would that affect the people who know you?

Love is the defining characteristic of being a true Christian. But as all of us know, there are some people that are harder to love than others. Can we agree that loving others is beyond our ability to do in our own strength? We need God's help and His power to love others as He loves us. Why don't we ask Him to empower us to love others and show us how to demonstrate that love? We don't need a jersey with God's name on it to show our love for Him. We can prove our love for Him by loving those around us.

Selah.

26

Draft Day

The first-year player draft, known as the Rule 4 Draft, is the primary method used by MLB teams to select new players. It is called the "Rule 4 Draft" because the procedures set forth for selecting the players are found in Rule 4 of the Major League Rules. The draft is held every June, and under the new collective bargaining agreement, there are 40 rounds to the draft. Since there are 30 MLB teams, this means that approximately 1200 amateur players are selected each year.

To be eligible for the draft, a player must:

1. Be a resident of the United States, Canada, or a U.S. territory;
2. Have never signed a major or minor league contract;
3. Have graduated high school if he has not attended college;
4. Be 21 years of age or completed his junior year if he is attending a 4-year college; all junior or community college players are eligible to be drafted at any time.[90]

Being eligible and being worthy to be drafted by a professional baseball team are two entirely different things. Each team employs scouts to find their next great player. Although the attributes they are looking for in a potential MLB player may vary, they are usually looking for a five-tool player. This is a player that has speed, hits for average, hits for power, can field, and has great arm strength. Finding a player who has all five attributes is a rare find. To put it in perspective, finding a

---

[90] registration.mlbpa.org/pdf/MajorLeagueRules.pdf

five-tool player would be comparable to finding a Mickey Mantle mint-condition baseball card in your attic that is worth thousands of dollars.

Scouts can generally recognize a professional-caliber player when they see one, but it would be an overstatement to say they always choose correctly. It boils down to an educated guess when they recommend to the team that a particular player be drafted in the early rounds. You can see from the following Hall of Fame list (or future Hall of Famer) that some of the greatest to play the game were overlooked in the early rounds of the draft. Apparently, they did not appear to the scouts to be Hall of Fame material.

1. Nolan Ryan (1965 draft)—295th selection/ 12th round[91]
2. Albert Pujols (1999 draft)—402nd selection/ 13th round[92]
3. Ryne Sandberg (1978 draft)—511th selection/ 20th round[93]
4. John Smoltz (1985 draft)—574th selection/ 22nd round[94]
5. Mike Piazza (1988 draft)—1,390th selection/ 62nd round[95]

There are other names that could be added to this list. The scouts are not to be faulted for failing to predict the future, but you can bet they regret overlooking these great players. The teams that failed to see the true potential in these five players hurt themselves for years to come.

---

[91] baseballreference.com/draft/?query_type=year_round&year_ID=1965&draft_round=12&draft_type=junereg
[92] baseball-almanac.com/players/player.php?=pujolal01
[93] baseball-almanac.com/players/player.php?=sandbry01
[94] baseball-almanac.com/players/player.php?=smoltjo01
[95] baseball-almanac.com/players/player.php?=piazzmi01

****

1 Samuel 16:1-13
Ephesians 1:3-4

How soon we are chosen is important to us. Do you remember those playground days at school when two kids picked their team members to play dodgeball, soccer, football or some other game? How did you feel when you were selected first? Second? Last?

To our surprise, this whimsical selection process did not cease to exist when we became adults. We feel special when we are selected from a pool of applicants to receive a college scholarship, a job promotion, or an opportunity to serve in public office. Conversely, we feel hurt or angry when we are overlooked or outright rejected by those making these decisions. Even if we are selected, it still hurts when we realize we were chosen not because of merit, but because there was no one else to choose from.

In the Old Testament, the Israelites wanted a king to lead them like the kings that led the nations surrounding them. The first king of Israel was Saul, and he looked the part. (1 Samuel 9:2). When Saul refused to follow God wholeheartedly, the prophet Samuel was sent to Bethlehem to anoint one of Jesse's sons as the next king. Samuel met with Jesse and his sons, but because Samuel was tempted to rely on mere appearance, he almost anointed the wrong son. In 1 Samuel 16:6-7, we read,

> "When they arrived, Samuel saw Eliab and thought, 'Surely the Lord's anointed stands here before the Lord.' But the Lord said to Samuel, 'Do not consider his appearance or his height, for I have rejected him. The Lord does not look at the things man looks at. Man looks at the outward appearance, but the Lord looks at the heart.'"

136

Fortunately for the Israelites, the clarity of God's voice persuaded Samuel to refrain from selecting someone based merely on appearance. Samuel obeyed God's voice and anointed Jesse's youngest son, David, as the next king.

When God chose you to follow Him, did He base that decision on how you looked in the scouting report? Did He base that decision on what you were or what you would become? We will see in a few moments that it was a blessing that God chose us not for what we were, but for what we would become.

In Ephesians 1:3-4, the apostle Paul states,

> "Praise be to the God and Father of our Lord Jesus Christ, who has blessed us in the heavenly realms with every spiritual blessing in Christ. For he chose us in him before the creation of the world to be holy and blameless in his sight."

How does it make you feel to know that God chose you before He even created the world? He did not choose you because you were the only one left to choose from. You were chosen by the God of all creation before the world and mankind were even in existence. That sounds a little more special than being the first pick in the first round of the MLB draft, doesn't it?

There are at least two things for us to consider. First, how many decisions have we made or are about to make that are based on appearance? In other words, are we making those decisions based on the present conditions or based on the potential we see? God did not choose us based on our present abilities, but He chose us while we were still sinners. If God saw our potential, then maybe we should look for the potential in others. What do you think?

Second, God has blessed us with every spiritual blessing we need to be holy and blameless in His sight. Do you feel holy and blameless? And yet, God's word says that is what you are if you have put your faith and life in Jesus' hands. Through Jesus and Jesus alone, we are holy and blameless.

Samuel was tempted to anoint the wrong son as the next king. Scouts are tempted to draft players based on their appearance. We are tempted to rely on our feelings to conclude we are unworthy and unholy. Samuel avoided disaster by listening to God's voice. We can do the same by allowing God's Word to determine what we believe rather than letting our feelings take us down the wrong path.

Selah.

27

Being Called Up

The goal of every minor league player is to be promoted to the major leagues and to stay there. It is not just the better pay, food, or accommodations that make being called up so desirable. It is the culmination of a life-long dream to play baseball at the highest level, and to compete against the best of the best. It is against this backdrop that in 2017, I met a minor league player who had recently been promoted from the minors to the major leagues.

The player was a minor league pitcher playing in the Los Angeles Angels organization. Our opportunity to meet occurred in the press box at a high school football game in the player's hometown. Like many professional baseball players, this player played other sports in high school besides baseball. I had seen him play several football games, but we had never met. He was being interviewed in the press box by a local radio announcer when he described what it was like to be in the major leagues. It is his story, and my impressions that will be described here. His real name will not be mentioned to respect his privacy. I will refer to him as Bill.

As Bill described his regimen of exercising, throwing, and running, it was clear to me that being a professional baseball player was not an occupation for a weak and undisciplined person. We think of starting pitchers as players that only play every five days, but we don't realize they put in a great deal of work on the days when they are not pitching. Bill went on to describe what it was like to pitch against some of the best players in baseball at Yankee Stadium and Fenway Park. When asked how he dealt with the pressure in those two environments, Bill commented that he thrived on the added pressure. Fear did not appear to be in Bill's vocabulary when it came to pitching. I was somewhat taken aback by the fierceness of Bill's competitive nature.

Finally, Bill was asked what it was like to play with Mike Trout and Albert Pujols. Bill had only good things to say about his teammates, but he did make some interesting comments. First, my impression of his approach in the clubhouse was to keep his head down, mind his own business, and speak only when spoken to. To me, Bill was not being rude or unfriendly. This was his way of showing respect for the veterans on the team. After all, Bill had only been in the major leagues a short time.

Second, Bill described one day when he was minding his own business and had his head in his locker when Mike Trout greeted him by name. It is hard to imagine how greeting someone by name could have such a profound effect on someone, but that was my impression of how Bill felt at that moment. When the future Hall of Famer called the rookie by name, it made Bill feel like he was part of the team and that he belonged in the major leagues. The sense of belonging, that you are good enough to play with the best players in the world, cannot be over-emphasized.

Finally, as I heard Bill speak of his time in the major leagues, it was immediately apparent that Bill was living a life that only a few ever experience. Bill had been in the presence of, played with, and personally talked to players that will one day be inducted into the Hall of Fame. These were players that knew Bill by name, and players Bill had the right to call by name. Bill had access to places and people that others could only dream about. Hearing Bill talk about these things left me with the impression that Bill was someone special. By special, I don't mean that he was better than or had more worth than any other person. He was special in the sense that I realized I was in the presence of someone who personally knew athletes that most of us only see on television or read about in sports articles.

****
Acts 4:13
Hebrews 4:14-16

Have you ever met someone who was famous or lived a life that seemed unattainable for the average person? How did that make you feel? Did you feel envious, unimportant, or angry? There were religious leaders that had a similar experience in the New Testament, and their reaction was one of surprise.

In Acts 3, Peter and John were on the way to the temple when they met a man crippled from birth. Peter commanded the man to walk, and he was instantly healed. In Acts 4, the religious leaders were disturbed by the message being preached by Peter and John so they had them arrested. The next day the leaders had Peter and John brought before them to answer for their message and conduct. After Peter courageously faced his accusers, we read in Acts 4:13 how Peter's response impacted the religious leaders.

> "When they saw the courage of Peter and John and realized that they were unschooled, ordinary men, they were astonished and they took note that these men had been with Jesus."

Peter and John were ordinary men who had been in extraordinary company. They had been with Jesus for three years in His public ministry. They knew Jesus by name, and He knew them by name. They were with Jesus when He performed miracles and preached the coming kingdom of God, and now Peter and John were continuing His work with the same courage and power that Jesus demonstrated. The

141

religious leaders were taken aback by the courage and power of Peter and John despite their lack of education. The only connection they could find to explain this courage was their relationship with Jesus.

Have you ever thought about your life as being mundane, routine, or a grind? Do you see yourself as just another nameless 'cog in the wheel' of life? If we feel this way, we could benefit from a few reminders of how special God thinks we are as believers in Christ. For the sake of brevity, I will only mention a few, but rest assured there are several more if you take the time to search your Bible for them:

1. Jesus chose you and calls you His friend (John 15:15-16);
2. You are part of a chosen people, a royal priesthood, a holy nation, a people belonging to God (1Peter 2:9);
3. You are sons of God and heirs of the promise God made to Abraham (Galatians 3:26-29); and
4. You have received the spirit of sonship and as a child of God, you can call God "Father" (Romans 8:15)

In my description of Bill's journey in the major leagues, it was mentioned that Bill had access to some of the greatest players of the game whether it was on the field or in the locker room. As believers, we have access to someone much greater than a future Hall of Famer. In Hebrews 4:14-16, we read,

> "Therefore, since we have a great high priest who has gone through the heavens, Jesus the Son of God, let us hold firmly to the faith we profess. For we do not have a high priest who is unable to sympathize with our weaknesses, but we have one who has been tempted in every way, just as we are—yet was without sin. Let us then approach the throne of grace with confidence, so that we may receive mercy and find grace to help us in our time of need."

There is one aspect to the believer's access to God that is sorely lacking in Bill's relationship with major league players that should be mentioned. Bill may personally know great ballplayers, but those players can't pitch or play the game for him. Bill has to earn his own way, or he will be sent back to the minors.

On the other hand, as a believer you not only have access to God, but you can receive the mercy and grace you need to do the work He has called you to do. You may not see your life as glamorous as a professional baseball player, but if you are doing God's will, then there is no higher calling than that.

Selah.

28

Arbitration and Free Agency

Arbitration and free agency have always been a mystery to me, but when you break it down, the goals for both are the same—a pay raise. A player becomes a free agent after having accumulated 6 years of major league service time. If his contract has expired, he can renegotiate with his current team or seek a better offer from another team.

The rules and procedures for arbitration are more voluminous, but don't get nervous. There are several detailed procedures in arbitration, but they will be summarized here for you. If you want to go into more detail, you can find the 2017-2021 collective bargaining agreement (CBA) between the teams and the Major League Baseball Players Association (MLBPA) on the internet.[96]

Generally, to be eligible for arbitration, a player must have between three and six years of major league service time. Before we go any further, keep in mind that an arbitration-eligible player already has a contract with a team that includes a specific salary. Except for those exceptional players with less than six years of service time, it is not uncommon for the owners of the team to pay their players as close as possible to the minimum salary required by the CBA. They do this to try to keep their payroll costs down.

In case you feel it is unfair to have an outstanding player with less than three years of service time being paid minimum wage, let me assure you that the minimum salary for major

---

[96] mlbplayers.com/pdf9/5450407.pdf

league players is not the minimum wage figure you have in mind. For 2019, the minimum salary for a major league player was $555,000, and that does not include other fringe benefits such as reimbursement for travel costs and meals.[97]

In an arbitration case, the salary dispute between the player and team is submitted to a panel of three arbitrators. The hearings are not open to the public, and they are held between February 1st and the 20th at an agreed-upon site with preference given to Los Angeles, Tampa/Orlando, or Phoenix. Evidence is offered by the player and the team, and after all the evidence has been submitted, the panel sets the salary at the amount proposed by either the player or the team. A decision should be made at the end of the hearing or within 24 hours.

The criteria considered by the arbitration panel in assessing the player's salary includes:

1. The player's contribution to his team which includes his overall performance, special qualities of leadership, and public appeal;
2. The length and consistency of his career contribution;
3. The record of his past compensation;
4. Comparable salaries from players with similar service time; and
5. The recent performance record of the team including the team standings and attendance records.[98]

When you review the five criteria, you may see that it is not too different from what your employer looks at when deciding if you deserve a raise. The criteria are essentially a report card on the player's total contribution to the team except for items 4 and 5 which the player has no control over. How would that

---

[97] Id.
[98] Id.

make you feel to know that you missed out on a raise because the competitor down the street pays his employees less than you get paid? It is the comparison of the salary and contributions between the player and other similarly-situated players that will be discussed in the next section. For now, take a breather. All that arbitration legalese can wear a person out.

****

Luke 18:9-14

We learn at an early age to compare ourselves with others. Children quickly point out to their parents that they are being unfairly treated if they are denied something that their siblings received. As they get older, they complain to their parents that everyone else in their class has a cell phone except them. We hear the same pleas when we talk about curfews, dating, and having a car.

The fallacy of comparing ourselves to others does not magically end when we pass from childhood to adulthood. As adults, aren't we guilty of the same thing? When was the last time you compared yourself to someone else at work and wondered why they were promoted instead of you? Have you found yourself comparing your assets to the assets of your neighbor down the street to bolster your sense of worth? How about comparing your family to another family to convince yourself that your family is somehow better than the other family?

It almost sounds incredible to even consider such thoughts, but do we subconsciously do this sort of thing from time to time? Do we even take this a step further and compare our relationship with God to others in our own church and wonder why someone else was selected to be an elder or lead a Bible study instead of us? As strange as that may seem, Jesus told a parable about two men who were in church where one was comparing his worth to the other. In Luke 18:9-14, we read,

> "To some who were confident of their own righteousness and looked down on everybody else, Jesus told this parable: Two men went up to the temple to pray, one a Pharisee and the other a tax collector. The Pharisee stood up and prayed about himself: 'God, I thank you that I am not like other men—robbers, evildoers, adulterers—or even like this tax collector. I fast twice a week and give a tenth of all I get.' But the tax collector stood at a distance. He would not even look up to heaven, but beat his breast and said, 'God, have mercy on me, a sinner.' I tell you that this man, rather than the other, went home justified before God. For everyone who exalts himself will be humbled, and he who humbles himself will be exalted."

Where did the Pharisee go wrong? By fasting twice a week and paying his tithe, it sounds like he was doing more than most people. But in this parable, is Jesus exposing the reason why we compare ourselves to others?

Is Jesus saying our motive for committing the sin of comparison is to make us feel superior to the one we are comparing ourselves to? More often than not, when we compare ourselves to someone else, aren't we the ones who come out on top and the other person is seen as falling short? If we find that to be true, it may be because we are exalting ourselves in our own eyes to make us feel better about ourselves. Could this be our attempt to ignore our faults or weaknesses instead of facing them?

The other point Jesus may be addressing here is how we are made righteous. In the Book of Romans, it tells us that righteousness is by faith, not by works. (Romans 4:2-3; 9:30-32; 10:4). The Pharisee's prayer is about himself and his accomplishments. The tax collector's prayer focused on God and His mercy. Possibly, if we listen to the prayers we are praying, it will reveal the condition of our hearts and what we truly believe.

How would you grade yourself when it comes to comparing yourself to others? Would you say 'Never, Sometimes, Most of the time, or All of the time?' If your answer is something other than 'Never,' then wouldn't it be wise to not stop there? Shouldn't we then ask ourselves the next question, specifically, 'What am I so insecure about that I feel I have to prove that I am better than someone else?' Once we answer that question, do you think we will put our finger on the problem? If we see what the problem is, we can then ask God to forgive us and help us find our security and worth solely in Him.

Baseball players in the arbitration process are trying to convince the arbitrators to set their salary at the amount they believe they are worth. They do this by comparing themselves to other players and argue they are better than, or at least, as good as someone else who has a salary near the salary they are seeking. They are exalting themselves to prove their worth.

We fall into the trap of doing the same thing. But we don't need to look for any additional evidence of our supreme worth other than Jesus Himself. He valued us so highly that He died on a cross so we could have a relationship with Him and an abundant life. What further evidence do we really need?

Selah.

29

The Locker Room

The locker room is more than a place where a player changes into his uniform before entering the playing field. It is a multi-purpose room that serves many different functions. In a way, it could be seen as a player's home away from home. Think about what you do in your home. You read, rest, sleep, listen to music, exercise, have serious and not so serious conversations, play games, pray, entertain, watch television, browse the internet, shower, and eat. These are the same activities that take place in a MLB locker room.

Except for members of the team, its staff, and representatives of the media, the locker room is essentially off-limits to everyone else. This makes good sense besides the obvious reason that players may be in varying states of undress. Like your home, the locker room is a place of refuge for players who spend at least 162 games in the public eye. It is intended to be a place where the players can relax, regroup, and get mentally and physically prepared to play the next game.

Although the locker room sounds like a fun place to be, there are times when problems arise outside the locker room that impact the atmosphere inside it. If a team is winning, the locker room is upbeat and there is peace on earth. If a team is losing or being criticized by the fans and the media, then questions arise about whether the team has the personnel and/or manager they need to win. Outside criticism can lead to self-doubt, blame, and disunity in the locker room. Professional baseball is a sport where trying isn't good enough. You either win or you lose your job. The pressure and adversity that a team goes through during a losing streak or losing season must be intense to say the least.

If you listen to the media when they interview a manager during a losing streak, it is not unusual to hear the manager say that even though the fans and media are unhappy, the team still believes in itself and is sticking together, or words to that effect. The manager is essentially telling the world that instead of believing the criticism, the team believes in itself and is determined to work together to win.

But criticism does not always come from outside sources. Sometimes its origin is from within the team itself. This is, by far, more serious and life-threatening to the team. We do not hear about dissension within a team very often. There may be two reasons for that. First, other than a personality conflict, it probably doesn't happen very often. Second, if it does exist, the team deals with it internally before it becomes public knowledge. Whether we hear about it or not, division within a baseball team cracks the winning foundation the team has labored to build. It is a recipe for disaster. It is so disastrous that if it cannot be resolved, the players that are causing the problem may be released or traded. Unity must be preserved at all costs or the season is lost.

****

Ephesians 4:1-6

How important is unity in your home, business, church, community, and nation? Since we sometimes fail to appreciate what we have until it's gone, let me ask that question a different way. What problems are created when there is dissension in your home, business, church, community, or nation? Dissension causes division, and division weakens or threatens the existence of the organization, whether that is something as small as a family or as large as a nation.

150

Why is unity so hard to achieve, and once obtained, why is it so hard to maintain? There are multiple answers you could give to both questions, but do you think we could generally explain it by saying that organizations are made up of imperfect people who have a free will, are prone to self-interest, and struggle with submission to authority?

It would be a mistake to underestimate the effect one person's self-interest and rebellion against authority can have on any organization if he chooses to exert his free will in that manner. Have you ever been in a meeting where one person, by his disrupting comments or behavior, defeats the purpose of having a meeting in the first place? If one person can cause such disruption, how hard would it be to maintain unity when you are dealing with a population of a city or nation? This may explain why some countries oppress their people and deny them the freedoms we enjoy in the U.S. If they can frighten their people into submission because of fear of punishment, then people won't exercise their free will and challenge those in authority when that is appropriate.

What about a group of people who care about each other such as a family or a church? Wouldn't it be easier to find and maintain unity there? Yes, it would be, but don't forget that even in your family or church, we continue to deal with imperfect people with a free will who struggle with self-interest and submission to authority. If we can never eliminate free will, self-interest, and our tendency to rebel, then how will we ever attain and maintain unity? We look to the Bible, and we ask for God's help. When Paul was in prison, he wrote these words in Ephesians 4:1-6:

> "As a prisoner for the Lord, then, I urge you to live a life worthy of the calling you have received. Be completely humble and gentle; be patient, bearing with one another in love. Make every effort to keep the unity of the Spirit through the bond of peace. There is one

body and one Spirit—just as you were called to one hope when you were called—one Lord, one faith, one baptism; one God and Father of all, who is over all and through all and in all."

Before I leave you to contemplate whether there is unity in your relationships and how you can promote that, there are three components to these verses that should be considered. First, how are we called to live? Since Christians are to be Christ-like, we should ask ourselves, 'How did Jesus live?' Did He freely choose to deny Himself and submit to His Father's will? Do we see any self-gratification or rebellion in Jesus' life? Following Jesus' example would be a good place for us to start when we consider how we are called to live.

Second, the qualities and actions that Paul urges his readers to strive for—humbleness, gentleness, patience, and love—are essential to maintaining unity. Paul also reminds his readers that it takes effort to have unity. We have to work at unity to find and keep it.

Third, Paul uses the word "one" no less than seven times in verses 4-6. Would it be fair to say that unity is not a problem when we are only dealing with one person? Is Paul suggesting here that instead of seeing different Christian denominations, we should see only one Christian Church? Don't all true Christians have faith in the same Savior? Don't we all serve the one true God who made us and is over us all? It would be disingenuous to say we have no differences, but don't we have more in common than we realize? Can you imagine the impact that a unified Christian Church would have? It would change the world.

Jesus said that a house divided against itself will fall (Luke 11:17). This principle applies to baseball teams and every other organization you can think of. Will we let division continue to run rampant in our families, churches, and nation, or will we do what we can where we are to promote unity? The choice is ours.

Selah.

30

RBIs

A triple crown winner for a position player in baseball is the player who leads his league in batting average, home runs, and runs batted in (RBIs). To show how difficult this is to accomplish, in the past 100-plus years that baseball has been played, there have only been 10 triple crown winners in the American league, and only 6 in the National league.[99] The last person to win the triple crown was Miguel Cabrera in 2012.[100]

To a hitter, the statistic that tabulates your RBI total is an important one. It is not just because RBIs are a part of the calculation for determining whether a player will be awarded the triple crown, but because scoring runs is what wins baseball games.

The basic goal of a baseball team is to win by scoring more runs than your opponent. When a player gets on base by walking, getting a hit, or because of a fielding error, it is the first step to scoring a run. The next step is for the players that follow to do whatever is necessary to move their teammate from first to second, from second to third, and from third to home. The goal is always to get the runners home, but it takes teamwork to do it. It is frustrating for the batter, the team, and the fans when the team has runners on base, but they fail to bring them home. When that happens with any degree of regularity, the team usually loses.

Who would you say had the most RBIs in a career? Was it Babe Ruth, Hank Aaron, Lou Gehrig, or Ty Cobb? The correct

---

[99] baseball-almanac.com/awards/aw_triph.shtml
[100] Id.

answer is Hank Aaron with 2,297.[101] He is closely followed by Babe Ruth who had 2,213.[102]

$$*\,*\,*\,*\,*\,*\,*$$

1Peter 1:8-9
1Corinthians 3:5-9

Have you ever thought about what is the goal of your faith? In baseball, the goal is to score more runs than your opponent. But what about our Christian faith? Is our goal to please God and have a relationship with Him? Is our goal to make it to heaven one day? Is it to be free of the guilt and shame associated with our sins? Is it to show others the path to peace and eternal life? Is it none of the above, some of the above, or all of the above?

In 1 Peter 1:8-9, the apostle Peter wrote about the believer's faith in Jesus by stating,

> "Though you have not seen him, you love him; and even though you do not see him now, you believe in him and are filled with an inexpressible joy, for you are receiving the goal of your faith, the salvation of your souls."

According to the apostle Peter, the goal of our faith is the salvation of our souls, the ultimate fulfillment of which only happens when we die unless Jesus returns before that. When we accept Jesus as our Lord and Savior and dedicate our lives to Him, it is as if we are now part of God's team. To continue with my baseball analogy, then what are we to do as a member of the team? We get ready to bat, and we do our best to drive in a run. What do I mean by that? We sow the seed to help bring about the salvation of a person's soul.

---

[101] baseball-almanac.com/hitting/hirbi1.shtml
[102] Id.

155

Hasn't God called all of us to know Him and make Him known to the world? We can know God by spending time with Him in prayer, Bible study, and with other like-minded believers. We can make Him known by sharing the gospel with others in word, deed, and by our lifestyle. Just as faith without works is dead so our gospel witness is ineffective unless we apply all three of these components—word, deed and lifestyle.

If we share the gospel in word only without supporting evidence of our faith by our deeds and lifestyle, we run the risk of being labeled a hypocrite. We will be deservedly criticized for not practicing what we preach.

On the other hand, if we share the gospel in deed and lifestyle only, we run the risk of taking credit for what is rightfully God's work in our lives. Others may praise us for being good people with high moral character when the truth is God is the One responsible for any goodness they see in us. Unless we explain who is responsible for our transformation, they will mistakenly attribute our admirable lifestyle to us rather than God's power and goodness. Can you see the importance of having all three components (word, deed, and lifestyle) when it comes to sharing the gospel?

No one person can reach all of the lost in our neighborhood, city, nation, or world, but each of us can do his or her part. It takes teamwork and God's help to accomplish such an enormous undertaking. It is not unlike baseball in that no one player usually brings all the baserunners home to win a game. Each player does his part to incrementally advance the runner until he scores a run. While addressing divisions within the church, the apostle Paul wrote about the role each person plays in sharing the gospel. In 1 Corinthians 3:5-9, we read,

> "What, after all, is Apollos? And what is Paul? Only servants, through whom you came to believe—as the Lord has assigned to each his task. I planted the seed,

Apollos watered it, but God made it grow. So neither he who plants nor he who waters is anything, but only God, who makes things grow. The man who plants and the man who waters have one purpose, and each will be rewarded according to his own labor. For we are God's fellow workers; you are God's field, God's building."

Paul acknowledges the role of those who share the gospel (plant the seed) and those who follow that up with additional teaching and instruction (water it), but his emphasis is on God who is the only One who can draw people to Christ. It takes dedication, teamwork, and unity of purpose to see the lost saved. Our job is to obey God by sharing the good news with others. God's job is to bring about the results. God will not do our job, and we can't do His.

Do you feel, like me, that sharing the gospel is better suited for someone else? It is not that we are too busy to do the job, but do you feel others are better equipped to convey the gospel in a more powerful and effective manner? If that is how we feel, then we may have misconstrued our responsibility. Our fear is that if we share the gospel with someone, the person may reject us and the message. But isn't this an example of us carrying the burden of seeing a positive outcome? Isn't that God's domain? He has taken the weight of that responsibility off our shoulders and put it on His own.

Sharing the gospel is a challenging and somewhat frightening thing to do at times, but we are not alone. We have God and a team of other believers to help us move the runner along and bring him home. If we ask for God's help in sharing the gospel, and take a step of faith, He will help us drive in a soul for the kingdom of God. That is the ultimate RBI.

Selah.

31

ITPHR

One of the more exciting plays you will see in baseball is when a player hits a ball inside the park, and he touches home plate before he is thrown out. We call this an inside the park home run (ITPHR). The player usually has no problem getting to third, but the excitement comes when he attempts to go home before the catcher can get the ball to tag him out. With each base that the runner passes, there is an increased risk he will be thrown out at the next base. More often than not, it is a close play at home plate with everyone holding their breath as they eagerly await the signal from the umpire calling the player out or safe. If he is out, it was nothing more than a lot of wasted effort. If he is safe, it is pure joy.

As you might expect, there are statistics showing who has the most ITPHRs in a career, a season, and in one game. If you were asked who had the most in these categories, it would be nearly impossible to guess so I won't ask. The career leader for ITPHRs is Jesse Burkett with 55.[103] Burkett played 16 years of professional baseball from 1890 to 1905.[104] The leader for most ITPHRs in a season is Sam Crawford who hit 12 in 1901. The leaders for most ITPHRs in a game are Guy Hecker who had 3 on August 15, 1886, and Tom McCreery who also had 3 on July 12, 1897. There are several players who have hit two ITPHRs in one game, but as of this writing, the last person to do so was Greg Gagne on October 4, 1986.[105]

****

---

[103] baseball-almanac.com/recbooks/rb_isphr.shtml
[104] baseball-almanac.com/players/player.php?=burkeje01
[105] baseball-almanac.com/recbooks/rb_isphr.shtml

This is the last chapter. As such, there will be a little more creative liberty here than in the previous chapters. A "parable" is defined as "usually a fictitious story that illustrates a moral attitude or a religious principle."[106] As you picture a player running the bases and heading home in an attempt to hit an inside the park home run, consider that each base represents a twenty-year segment of your life. The 90 feet from home plate to first base represents your age from birth to age 20. The next 90 feet represents your age from 20 to 40. The distance from second to third base represents your age from 40 to 60. Finally, you age another 20 years from third base to home plate where your life ends. Keep in mind that there is no stopping on a base or between bases. If you are tempted to stop running, for instance, between first and second base when you are 30 years old, this parable will not allow that. Remember, you are trying to hit an inside the park home run. No one stops running until they reach home plate.

For a moment, remember where you were and what you were doing when you were on first (20 yrs. old), second (40 yrs. old), or third (60 yrs. old) base or anywhere in between. Would you want to go back to the previous base? If so, then why? Keep in mind that if you want to go back or stay on a certain base indefinitely, that is not allowed. Time forces us to run the bases of life. What should our attitude be as we are driven by time to the next base not fully knowing what to expect?

In the book of 1 Timothy, Paul writes to Timothy, his young assistant, to carry on the work in Ephesus while Paul was in Macedonia. Paul urges and encourages Timothy to stay true to his mission, and it is those words that I want to use as we conclude this study. In 1 Timothy 6:11-16, we read,

---

[106] merriam-webster.com/dictionary/parable

"But you, man of God, flee from all this, and pursue righteousness, godliness, faith, love, endurance, and gentleness. Fight the good fight of the faith. Take hold of the eternal life to which you were called when you made your good confession in the presence of many witnesses. In the sight of God, who gives life to everything, and of Christ Jesus, who while testifying before Pontius Pilate made the good confession, I charge you to keep this command without spot or blame until the appearing of our Lord Jesus Christ, which God will bring about in his own time—God, the blessed and only Ruler, the King of kings and Lord of lords, who alone is immortal and who lives in unapproachable light, whom no one has seen or can see. To him be honor and might forever. Amen."

As we go through life, would we be wise to obey the four precepts outlined in these verses?

1. Flee and pursue: We run from one thing, and toward another. We run from the former things that bound us in sin, some of which are named in verses 3-10. We run toward a life that is characterized by righteousness, godliness, faith, love, endurance, and gentleness.
2. Fight: We are in a spiritual battle whether we realize it or not. We need to look no further than the Book of Job to understand that sometimes bad things happen because we are being attacked by the enemy. But the battle to maintain our faith in God is a fight that is worth the struggle. Your faith in God is your most valuable possession. Without it, you cannot please God or have any hope of eternal life with Him.
3. Maintain a firm grip on your salvation: It is our salvation that guarantees our eternal life. There may be times when we feel unworthy and unrighteous, but our salvation is not based on feelings. It is based on the written and living Word of God, Jesus Christ. If you have

chosen the path to eternal life as described in the Bible, then hold firmly to that despite your feelings.

4. Endure until Jesus returns: Life on earth can be complicated and difficult, but with God's help, we can endure whatever life throws at us and live above our circumstances. True peace and joy are only found in a relationship with Jesus Christ because it is only then that we can see the temporal nature of the things of this world. It is transforming to know with certainty what lies ahead at the end of your life. You know the feeling you have when you know the outcome of an important game with a divisional opponent before you ever watch the game. You watch the game in perfect peace knowing that even though it looks bad for your team going into the bottom of the 9th inning, your team will end up winning the game. As long as we, as believers, never lose sight of what awaits us in eternity, enduring until Jesus returns will be made much easier.

As all of us know, life is uncertain. The parable of running the bases used in this chapter suggests that we will live to be 80 years of age, but there is no guarantee we will live past today much less until we are 80. Knowing this should create a sense of urgency within us.

If something in our lives is left undone, such as a broken relationship, shouldn't we try to fix it today since our tomorrow may never come? Putting off until tomorrow what we could do today to reconcile a relationship is risky business. We cannot change the past, but we can, with God's help, secure a brighter future. In a race, it is not where we stand at the midway point that matters. It is where we finish that counts. Run the race with endurance that God has set before you and finish well.

Selah.

Made in the USA
Columbia, SC
16 April 2024

34468319R00100